ANTHROPOLOGY RESEARCH AND DEVELOPMENTS

'CRIMINAL TRIBE' TO 'PRIMITIVE TRIBAL GROUP' AND THE ROLE OF WELFARE STATE

THE CASE OF LODHAS IN WEST BENGAL, INDIA

ANTHROPOLOGY RESEARCH AND DEVELOPMENTS

Additional books in this series can be found on Nova's website under the Series tab.

Additional e-books in this series can be found on Nova's website under the e-book tab.

ANTHROPOLOGY RESEARCH AND DEVELOPMENTS

'CRIMINAL TRIBE' TO 'PRIMITIVE TRIBAL GROUP' AND THE ROLE OF WELFARE STATE

THE CASE OF LODHAS IN WEST BENGAL, INDIA

SANTANU PANDA
AND
ABHIJIT GUHA

nova publishers
New York

Library of Congress Cataloging-in-Publication Data

ISBN: 978-1-63463-685-8

Published by Nova Science Publishers, Inc. † New York

This book is dedicated to
Chuni Kotal the first Lodha graduate of India,
a student of the Department of Anthropology, Vidyasagar University

CONTENTS

FOREWORD

Ethnographic accounts, no matter how much flexible may they outwardly appear in their approaches to study, style of narratives, as well as extent of coverage, are by and large based on intensive field investigations hitherto least appreciated. The problem of such an exercise really becomes crucial, when the investigator has to deal with primitive tribal communities. *'Criminal Tribe' to 'Primitive Tribal Groups' and the Role of Welfare State: The Case of the Lodhas in West Bengal* by Santanu Panda and Abhijit Guha, as the title as such suggests, is the account of an officially identified 'primitive tribe' who for about a century had to live with the ignominy of being ascribed with a 'Criminal tribe ' tag. As the authors painstakingly dig deep into the records of facts, what becomes apparent is the peoples' determination to ignore what the so-called rulers prescribed as the laws of the land and they went on fighting an unequal but undaunted battle against such imposition. Whether the people ever realized the authority of a State to legitimize its own action is not the major issue.

Ethnography, by strict anthropological definition, is the study of individual cultures, primarily descriptive and non-interpretative in nature. Accordingly, the present narrative is ethnography with a difference. It describes, analyses, and tries to interpret, examining the facts of life of the concerned people 'in space and time'.

Allan R. Holmberg's monograph: *Nomads of the Long Bow: The Siriono of Eastern Bolivia,* is also an account of a primitive tribal people, which because of the very nature of livelihood of the Siriono as well as the inherent quality of the discourse, assumed the character of a classical ethnographic literature. Lauriston Sharp considered it as the typical illustration of "… Paleolithic Ethnography". As we are able to see through the descriptions of an 'eyewitness' ethnographer: the world-view, culture, behavior, and the overall style of life of the Siriono appear to be tuned to a rhythm scarcely fathomed. Thus their time stands still. Technically speaking, even being part of a modern nation-state, the people present the picture of total indifference about the existence of civilizations. Literary imaginations aside, the snap-shots of the Siriono way of life has hardly many parallels known from anywhere in the world.

'Criminal Tribe' to 'Primitive Tribal Groups' and the Role of Welfare State: The Case of the Lodhas in West Bengal is also an account of a people who, as already indicated, even before being designated as the 'Primitive Tribal Group' had to pass through a derogatory identity: the 'Criminal Tribe'. Traditionally, gatherer-hunters though, they in no way represent a style of life resembling that of any stone-age people. As we appreciate through the descriptions of Panda and Guha, they live in close proximity to agricultural farmers though, are not sufficiently at home in that art. They feel more comfortable in gathering than in growing food. Their relative indifference in possessing livestock and toward agricultural farming, including possession of farm land s, speaks of a value that the modern world can perhaps never fully gauge. Nevertheless, the evident apathy they are meted out does not disturb them at all. A close watch of their gathering pattern demonstrates their inclination to live in the world of trust.

The Lodhas are not totally unaware about the existence of States or Nation-States but prefer to be away from the contemporary style of living. The rich data generated by Panda and Guha suggests the need for understanding the 'language of indifference', 'language of silence', 'language of apathy '. As implied in their account, until then, all developmental initiatives of the welfare state s are certain to meet with indifferent results. After all, a distrust that appears to have been deliberately crafted to create a distance between the state and the people cannot be undone by mere pious wishes.

By definition, a state has the right to rule and to bring about transformations in the life-style of the concerned people, but at whose cost ? Should the Lodhas welcome such initiatives, even if they mean sapping off the levels of their confidence? The people, as the narration suggests, despite their awareness about the authority and power of the state, prefer to live as the care-free children of Mother Nature. Those who can withstand injustice, hunger, discrimination, and ridicule at relative ease, those who do not fear to be outwitted, perhaps have nothing to lose. This is precisely the reason that the Lodhas, even being citizens of a state, are immensely capable in many respects like non-state people to deny the existence of the state. This very fact brings them close to the Siriono, whose apparently resigned life-style virtually speaks of their indifference about the existence of states.

The volume makes an immensely enjoyable reading.

Ajit Kumar Danda, Ph.D. (Cornell), FNASc.
Chairman, Indian National Confederation and
Academy of Anthropologists (INCAA)
Former Director, Anthropological Survey of India
and Professor, Asiatic Society, Kolkata, India
E-mail: akdanda@hotmail.com

PREFACE

This is a problem focused and applied study regarding the impact of various development inputs (e.g., land distribution, housing, solar energy, rainwater harvesting, domestic animal etc.) given and monitored by the governmental and non-governmental agencies to a small, economically backward and socially marginalized scheduled tribe of West Bengal named Lodha. The scheduled tribe has recently been categorised by the Government as a 'Primitive Tribal Group' (PTG).The marginalization of this tribal community has a historical background which has been explored in the introductory chapter of the book.

The empirical survey for the study was conducted in three administrative blocks, viz. Binpur II, Nayagram and Narayangargh within the administrative boundary of the Paschim (West) Medinipur district of West Bengal state of India. The impact of the developmental inputs in this research has been studied empirically through anthropological fieldwork at three levels.

At the first level, all the developmental inputs were enlisted in the selected study areas along with the collection of basic socio-demographic and economic data.

The second level of enquiry dealt with the analysis and interpretation of field data on the actual utilization of the enlisted developmental inputs which were collected along with views of the beneficiary community in the selected field areas.

At the third level, an attempt has been made to assess the impact of the various developmental inputs by comparing the developmental scenario in the three selected areas which also provided an opportunity to study the variation within the same community in terms of utilization of the development inputs in the three different locations of the same district within the state of West Bengal. At this level, an attempt has also been made to recommend some measures for the better utlilisation of development inputs for the socioeconomic improvement of the Lodhas of Paschim Medinipur in West Bengal.

This study has both practical and policy relevance since Central and State Governments have sanctioned different schemes for the overall development of the Lodhas of West Bengal. Interestingly, the implementation of these schemes suffered setback in various places of West Bengal. There has been very few or almost no attempt to assess the reasons behind the failures towards the implementations these developmental inputs among the Lodhas.

This research is designed specifically to assess the impact of development programmes among the Lodhas. In this study we have also made an attempt to point out some of the basic problems towards the implementation of developmental schemes planned and executed by the respective departments of the State and local self Government s designated as Panchayat.

Finally, with the findings of this study, we have made an attempt to suggest certain measures which may be adopted by the Government for the successful implementation of the developmental inputs for the improvement of the socio-economic and living conditions of this small and marginalised community of West Bengal.

Santanu Panda and Abhijit Guha
Panda9732@yahoo.in;
abhijitguhavuanthro@rediffmail.com
Department of Anthropology
Vidyasagar University, Midnapore
West Bengal, India.

About the Authors

Santanu Panda b. 1978, earned his Master's degree in 2003 and Ph.D in Anthropology from Vidyasagar University, West Bengal, India in 2013. Awarded Research Scholarship under the Research Fellowship in Science for Meritorious Students (RFSMS) by the University Grants Commission, India. At present working as Indian Council of Social Science Research (ICSSR), Post Doctoral Fellow attached with the Department of Anthropology, Vidyasagar University. Dr. Panda completed his Ph.D. on a problem focused and applied study on the impact of various development inputs (e.g., land distribution, housing, solar energy, rainwater harvesting, domestic animal etc.) given and monitored by the governmental and non-governmental agencies to a small, economically backward and socially marginalized scheduled tribe of West Bengal named Lodha. He is engaged in development oriented research on Lodhas for more than a decade. Also worked as research investigator in a Research Project entitled 'Exclusion of Muslim outcastes in West Bengal'

sponsored by ICSSR under the supervision of Professor Abhijit Dasgupta, Department of Sociology, Delhi School of Economics, Delhi University. To date, Dr. Panda has published 17 articles in various International and National level peer-reviewed journals (viz. *Tribal Tribune*, *Journal of the Indian Anthropological Society*, *South Asian Anthropologist*, *International Journal of Research in Sociology and Social Anthropology, Global Journal of Human Social Science, Tribal Health Bulletin, North Bengal Anthropologist)* and edited volumes, and presented papers in Seminars, Conferences and workshops in India. He also acted as peer reviewer in the *Journal of Anthropology*, New York and *Development Education Journal,* Philippines. He is also an editorial board member in the *Development Education Journal.* Life member of the Indian Anthropological Society (IAS), Kolkata, Indian National Confederation and Academy of Anthropologists (INCAA), India and International Society for Development and Sustainability (ISDS), Japan.

ABHIJIT GUHA b. 1956. M.Sc., Anthropology (1983) and M.Phil., Environmental Science (1984), University of Calcutta, India. Awarded ICSSR doctoral fellowship attached with the Centre for Studies in Social Sciences, Calcutta during 1984-85. Conducted anthropological research on Bengali Kinship under the supervision of Professor Surajit Sinha, former Vice-Chancellor of Viswa Bharati University. Currently, teaching at the Anthropology Department of Vidyasagar University since 1986 and completed his Ph.D. in Anthropology from Vidyasagar University in 2002 on the various adverse impacts of land acquisition on the pro-peasant policies of the Left Front Government in West Bengal. He is engaged in displacement, resettlement and rehabilitation research for the last 15 years and has worked with Walter Fernandes in a project on West Bengal and was associated with the Postgraduate diploma course on Participatory Management of

Resettlement and Rehabilitation at the School of Social Sciences, IGNOU, New Delhi. Guha was one of the supervisors of a collaborative and interdisciplinary research project on the Oral History of the peasant Women's Organizations sponsored by the Centre for Women's Development Studies, New Delhi. He has published about more than 100 articles, comments, and book reviews in various International and National level peer-reviewed journals, newspapers and edited volumes which included *Current Anthropology*, *Population and Development Review*, *Economic and Political Weekly*, *European Journal of Development Research*, *Anthropological Forum*, *Social Change*, *Sociological Bulletin*, *South Asian Anthropologist*, *Mainstream*, *Frontier*, *Journal of the Indian Anthropological Society* and *Journal of Human Ecology*. Presented papers in Seminars, Conferences and workshops in India and abroad. He was University Grants Commission visiting fellow at the Department of Sociology, Delhi School of Economics, Delhi University, Centre for Advanced Study in Anthropology, Utkal University and also taught Law and Anthropology in the West Bengal National University of Juridical Sciences, Kolkata. Guha has written a book *Land, Law and the Left: The Saga Disempowerment of the Peasantry in the Era of Globalization* (2007), Concept Publishing Company, New Delhi. Dr. Guha has supervised a research project sponsored by the Planning Commission of the Government of India on the socioeconomic impact assessment of the governmental development programmes implemented among the Lodha/Sabar community in West Bengal in which Dr. Santanu Panda was a co-researcher.

ACKNOWLEDGMENTS

At the outset, we convey our heartiest gratitude to all the villagers particularly the Lodhas of the study area who despite their hardship and trouble helped us by giving information on the development inputs which were given by the Government. We owe our enormous debts to Kanchan Digar former Pradhan of Makarampur Gram Panchayat and till now a member of the women Self-Help-Group (SHG) who spared her valuable time to provide useful information to the first author on the functioning of SHGs and implementation of the developmental programmes. We also acknowledge the cooperation of Bidhan Kotal, Secretary of the Village Development Committee of Daharpur who supplied official information regarding the development schemes and their implementation to the first author.

We are greatly indebted to Daman Bhakta, Pradhan of Patina Gram Panchayat of Singhdhui village at Nayagram block who introduced the first author as a researcher to the villagers and also for providing accommodation in the village.

Our heartiest thanks to Dusmanta Nariala, District Magistrate, who sponsored a project on the impact assessment of the developmental programme among the Lodhas in Binpur II and Nayagram blocks of Paschim Medinipur to the second author in which we first began our research on the utilization of the development inputs given to the Lodhas of Binpur II and Nayagram blocks of Paschim Medinipur district. We also express gratitude to the officials and the staff of the Paschim Medinipur district administration for extending their help and cooperation to conduct the research. Our heartiest thanks to the Block Development Officers (BDO) of the three administrative blocks and as well as the employees of the Gram Panchayat s offices.

We are grateful to the Librarian of the Anthropological Survey of India, Kolkata for giving us access to use the books and journals in the reading room of the library. We also express our acknowledgements to the Librarian and the staff of the Central Library of the Vidyasagar University.

We are greatly indebted to Professor Ajit Kumar Danda, who was kind to write the foreword of the book by spending some of his valuable time from his busy schedule.

We also express our sincerest gratitude to Professor Kaushik Sankar Bose, Faculty of the Department of Anthropology, Vidyasagar University for his kind academic advice and moral support towards this research and continuous insistence to write the book. Professor Bose first introduced us to the NOVA publishing Company.

We are also grateful to the University Grants Commission (UGC) for providing financial assistance in the form of a Research Scholarship under the Research Fellowship in Science for Meritorious Students (RFSMS) during 2009-2012 which helped the first author to complete his Ph.D thesis on the Lodhas.

We are grateful to Professor Ranjan Chkrabarti, the Vice-Chancellor and Dr. Ranajit Dhar, the then Registrar of Vidyasagar University to recommend the application of the first author for a Post Doctoral Fellowship sponsored by the Indian Council for Social Science Research (ICSSR). We are also grateful to ICSSR for providing financial support to the first author in the form of a Post Doctoral Fellowship under which the research on the Lodhas could be continued. We also owe a lot to the anonymous examiners of the Ph.D. thesis of the first author who recommended it for publication.

I would like to thank Professor Pradip Kumar Bhowmick Professor Indian Institute of Technology (IIT), Kharagpur and Dr. Manoranjan Bhowmick, Superintendent of Institute of Social Research and Applied Anthropology (ISRAA) for providing useful information regarding the history and the present activities of the institution related to the developmental programmes undertaken by the institute for the Lodhas of Daharpur village.

Our special thanks go to Dr. Rajat Kanti Das, former Professor and UGC Emeritus Fellow, Department of Anthropology, Vidyasagar University, Dr. Jayanta Sarkar former Joint Director, Anthropological Survey of India, and Dr. Satyabrata Chakrabarti former Deputy Director Anthropological Survey of India for providing valuable academic inputs towards the completion of the Ph.D thesis of the first author without which this book could not have been written.

Our heartiest thanks to Dr. Dipak Kumar Midya, Head of the Department, Department of Anthropology, Vidyasagar University and also Professor

Falguni Chakrabarty for their kind cooperation in the Department to continue the research work.

We also like to thank Dr. Samiran Bisai, Dr. Asish Das and Dr. Raja Chakrabarty, senior research scholars of the Department of Anthropology for constantly inspiring the first author to complete his Ph.D. thesis without which this book could not have been written.

We convey our sincerest thanks to all the research scholars of the Department of Anthropology for the technical support while we worked for the Ph.D thesis of the first author. Our special thanks to Dr. Sadaruddin Biswas, Arup Majumder and Subhamay Kisku for their continued interest towards the completion of the thesis.

We are grateful to Shyam Sundar Roy, Midnapore Correspondent for *The Statesman*, Kolkata and Tapas Maity, editor *Upatyaka*, a local daily for writing news articles about our research on the Lodhas.

The first author would like to express his warmest thanks to his wife Rubi who continuously insisted to complete the thesis and the book. He also acknowledges the love and affection of his parents for their support towards the continuation of his higher study without which neither the Ph.D thesis nor the book could have been written. The first author is also greatly indebted to his little son, Sayandeep, who often had to bear the pains of prolonged absence of his father.

Last but not the least, we thank Carra Feagaiga of the Nova Science Publishers, Inc. of USA for taking all the troubles to review our book proposal and our thanks are also due to the anonymous reviewers of NOVA for their useful suggestions to improve the draft manuscript of the book. All the shortcomings of the book which still remain lie with us.

ABBREVIATIONS AND ACRONYMS

BLLRO	Block Land and Land Reforms Department
BDO	Block Development Officer
BPL	Below poverty Line
CPI(M)	Communist Party of India (Marxist)
DHDR	District Human Development Report
GP	Gram Panchayat
IAY	Indira Awas Yojana
ISRAA	Institute of Social Research and Applied Anthropology
ICDS	Integrated Child Development Scheme
LFG	Left Front Government
MGNREGA	Mahatma Gandhi National Rural Employment Guarantee Act
MT loan	Mid-Term Loan
NGO	Non Government Organization
NH	National Highway
PTG	Primitive Tribal Group
PMGSY	Pradhan Mantri Gram Swarojgar Yojana
RSVY	Rastriya Sama Vikas Yojana
SHG	Self-Help-Group
SGRY	Sampoorna Grameen Rozgar Yajana
ITDP	Integrated Tribal Development Project

SUMMARY

Chapter I

The history of the Lodha tribe is the story of exploitation, marginalization, human right s violation, social exclusion and policy failures on the part of the Government s to deliver social and economic justice to a group of voiceless people who were categorized by the colonial Government as 'Criminal Tribe' and then by the Independent Government as 'Denotified' and 'Primitive Tribal Group'. Does 'social harmony ' and 'inclusive development' bear significant meaning without the inclusion of this ethnic minority in the mainstream of a democratic country? Lodhas of West Bengal is one such community which has a long history of marginalization and oppression by the state and the dominant communities and they also have a history of demarginalization which had started in the post colonial period by the efforts of the state and non-state actors as well as the members of the community themselves. In this book an attempt has been made to look into the twin process of marginalization vis-à-vis demarginalization of the Lodhas who are listed as a scheduled tribe in India.

Chapter II

The Lodhas are now treated as one of the denotified communities by the Central Government. In West Bengal, Lodhas are mainly concentrated in the districts of Paschim (West) Medinipur and Purba (East) Medinipur. As mentioned earlier, in the pre-Independence period they were treated as a Criminal Tribe till the revocation of the Criminal Tribes Act in 1952. The Census of 1981 shows that the total population of the Lodhas including the Kharias and the Kherias of West Bengal is 53,718. The Lodhas are concentrated in Midnapore District and their total number according to the Census of 1981 was 16,534. Besides West Bengal, they are also found in the Mayurbhanj and Baleswar districts of Orissa (now Odisha). Originally, they inhabited hilly rugged terrains covered with jungle. Their mother tongue is Lodha, which is close to Savara, an Austro-Asiatic language. They are fluent in Bengali. Traditionally they were forest dwellers but now they have started cultivation either as owner or as agricultural labourer and are also engaged in hunting and fishing. At present the Lodhas do not live exclusively in the forest covered areas, but have spread out in other deforested regions and are found to work there as agricultural and non-agricultural labourers. Over the decades, the Lodhas gradually changed their occupation from hunting gathering to agriculture as an alternative means of livelihood owing to deforestation.

Chapter III

Under the general background of the state of West Bengal and the Paschim (west) Medinipur district, the villages in the study area have been described. It was found that almost all the villages (except one in the Narayangarh block) inhabited by the Lodhas were located near forests with poor transport facilities. In majority of the villages the Lodha families were found to depend on forest product collection, although in some villages it was found that agriculture was being practiced. The supply of drinking water facilities, sanitation and health care delivery systems were found to be in poor condition in most of the Lodha villages. We have also described the age -sex composition, sex-ratio, household size, marital status, subsistence pattern and literacy condition among the Lodhas separately in the three blocks The findings on basic socio-demographic features showed a preponderance of females in almost all the age). This fact is most revealing in all the young age groups from 0-4 up to 35-39.The marital status shows, the females are found to marry at an early age than the males. The literacy status shows that the overall literacy condition is not very satisfactory (43.35 %) and the condition of the females in this regard is worse than the males. The literacy condition of the population also revealed that the younger Lodhas have achieved more primary education than the older persons. The household size of the Lodhas in the surveyed population revealed a predominance of small households. The subsistence pattern of the study area revealed that the Lodhas in the study area were mostly engaged in forest produce collection and they were also found to be working as labourers in the agricultural and non-agricultural sectors.

Chapter IV

Although the chief aim of the Government was to bring the Lodhas in the fold of agriculture and settle them like a group of farmers, the distribution of land by the Land and Land Reforms Department to the landless Lodha families largely remained an unfinished task. It was found that 41 percent of the Lodha families in the study received some kind of development inputs from the Government. Our findings further revealed that at the time of our survey 402(29.09%) beneficiary families out of 1382 have received various types of developmental inputs in different combinations. The nature of distribution of developmental inputs by the Government showed that emphasis was given to cash loan for house building and high technology solar cells. Through our observation and interviews with the beneficiaries we have found that most of the houses were built in a hurried manner and seemed to be weak in structure. The beneficiaries also expressed their dissatisfaction with the newly built houses. We have also found that the majority of the beneficiaries who received solar cells either sold them against cash to well-to-do neighbours belonging to other communities or could not use them properly. A comparative assessment of the development inputs in the three administrative blocks revealed that the utilization of development inputs was extremely poor in Binpur-II block while inputs were most successfully utilized in the Narayangarh block. Nayagram lies in the middle position in terms of the utilization of the development inputs.

Chapter V

An attempt to compare the utilization pattern of the four major development inputs, viz. (i) land distribution, (ii) house construction,(iii) distribution of solar cells and (iv) distribution of cattle, given to the Lodhas in the study area have been made. Overall, the comparative scenario of the utilization of the four major development inputs in the three blocks among the Lodhas showed a marked variation. Variation in utilization performance is also found in terms of the type of development input. The development inputs given to the Lodhas have been utilized by them most successfully in the Narayangarh block and interestingly, solar plates have not been given at all in this block. The worst scenario is found in the Binpur-II block in which non-utilization of all the development inputs predominated the scene. Nayagram lies in the middle position in terms of the utilization of the development inputs. When we look separately to each development input, it was found that the utilization of domestic cattle can be regarded as a kind of development input which turned out to be an unutilized one except among the Lodhas of Narayangarh who showed the best performance in the utilization of all the inputs. The utilization of financial assistance for house construction given as a development input showed that even the overall worst performers (Lodhas of Binpur-II) have made a substantial utilization of house construction as a development input. Regarding *patta* land, we do not find full utilization in the blocks but in case of house we find full utilization in Narayangarh The development assistance given in the form of cattle revealed a grim scenario both at Binpur II and Nayagram blocks while the performance of the beneficiaries towards the utilization of this input was found to be fairly well in Narayangarh block.

Chapter VI

The Lodhas are regarded as a marginalized and economically backward tribe and both the Central and the State Government s have allocated funds under various development schemes to improve the socioeconomic condition of the tribe since Independence. The condition of the tribe however did not improve considerably, although, various development inputs were given to this marginalized tribe. Under this background this field based anthropological research has been carried out to make an assessment of the ground realities of the situation regarding the socioeconomic and demographic condition of the Lodhas and also the scenario around the implementation of the development inputs given to them under the governmental schemes in three administrative blocks of Paschim Medinipur district of West Bengal. In this work, we have found differences in terms of the utilization of the development inputs by the Lodha families of the three administrative blocks of Paschim Medinipur district. The findings of this research revealed that the Lodha settlement of Binpur-II block suffered from poor communication and transport, and lack of access to the political leaders and panchayat members of the area although the local panchayat leader belonged to their own community. The Government has not yet been able to organise skill development programmes for the Lodha women and men of this block.

In Nayagram block, the Lodhas were found to be in better condition than they were in Binpur-II, in terms of communication and access to local panchayat leadership. Here the Government had also taken up some programmes through an NGO to monitor the implementation of the development inputs.

In Narayangarh block, the Lodhas also seemed to be more aware about the development inputs than their counterparts in the other blocks studied in this research. They also owned cultivable land and got training in agriculture and other skill development training programmes organised jointly by an NGO and the state Government. Finally we recommended that one should identify the ground reality of the poor and economically backward community for the improvement of their socio-economic conditions. Two things should be given utmost priority. The road transport and public communication systems should be improved in all the blocks, particularly in Binpur II and Nayagram. Governmental efforts towards the supply of safe drinking water and minor irrigation systems should be initiated immediately in all the areas inhabited by the Lodhas and last but not the least the economy of this marginalized community should be reconstructed on the basis of a combination of forest based agriculture which would fit them into their tradition and culture.

LIST OF TABLES

List of Figures

Chapter I

INTRODUCTION

Budhan a 28-year-old from Akarbaid village in Purulia,[1] one of the poorest districts in West Bengal, was arrested on 10 February 1998. He was a member of the 'Denotified Tribe' named 'Kheria Sabar' (also known as Lodhas[2] in West Bengal) was arrested by police and brutally tortured within the police custody for seven days and he died in custody. The police, however reported that he committed suicide by hanging himself in the lock-up. Later, Paschim Bangya Kheria Sabar Kalyan Samiti, a civil rights organization filed a writ petition in Calcutta High Court against the police (Writ Petition No.3715 dated 1998) and it was revealed that Budhan was killed by police torture. (*Amnesty International Report*, 2001:24). Ganesh Devy, a litterateur and social activist vividly narrated in her article the case of the death of Budhan Sabar in police custody in February, 1998. (Devy, 2000: 53-55). Justice Rama Pal of the Calcutta High Court rejected the police story in the judgment delivered and ordered the State Government to pay compensations of Rs. 80,000/- to his wife and Rs. 5,000/- to his parents. The judgment also

---

[1] Purulia district is one of the twenty districts of West Bengal state in Eastern India. The town of Purulia is the administrative headquarters of the district.(Wikipedia accessed through Google on 17.10.2014)

[2] The wikipedia says, 'Lodha means piece of flesh named after their ancestor. Lodhas have been in the focus of anthropologists and social activists.During the early period of their rule, the British government in India oppressed the tribal people of Jungle Mahal s, who were traditionally dependent upon the forests for a living. They had revolted but were ruthlessly suppressed. Having been deprived of their livelihood and without any alternatives, they took to criminal ways of life and were subsequently branded a criminal tribe. They should properly be labelled as uprooted rebels. Lodha titles are Nayek, Mallick, Digar, Sardar, Bhokta, Kotal, Dandapat, Bhunya etc. These titles reflect social responsibility. They are descendants of Jarasandh from Mahabharata. The Lodhas hold that they are Sabars. (http://en.wikipedia.org/wiki/Lodha_people accessed through Google on 21.10.2014).

directed the State to punish the Jail Superintendent of Purulia and the office in-charge of Burrabazar police station.

In 2004, an awful incident occurred among the Lodhas during the Left Front Government [3] regime at Amlasole village in Paschim (West) Medinipur District. Media reported the starvation death of five Lodha -Sabars in a village named Amlasole in Binpur II in Paschim (West) Medinipur in the state in the year 2004. Later, these deaths of Lodha-Sabar individuals owing to hunger and malnutrition raised uproar in West Bengal Assembly. At that time the then Chief Minister of West Bengal, Mr. Buddhadev Bhattacharjee, did accept that 'conditions of starvation' existed not only in Amlasole but in many other villages although his party remained convinced that the deaths were due to disease caused by malnutrition and lack of basic medical care. The communist led State Government denied that lack of food could have led to death of the individuals of this marginalized ethnic group. The Government sent a medical team which concluded that the deaths occurred among the Lodhas owing to their excess consumption of illegal liqueur and incidence of diseases like Tuberculosis, Jaundice and Malaria. The disturbing fact however remained that the area where the Lodhas died did not have any road connectivity, proper health care delivery system and the governmental food distribution system through Public Distribution Shop was in a very poor condition. (*Economic and Political Weekly*, 2004:2541). A vivid firsthand account of the District Magistrate, Mr. Chandan Sinha also matched with the EPW report. In addition Mr.Sinha concluded:

> .... Amlasole became a metaphor for starvation deaths in rural India, of extreme deprivation, of neglect. Yet, most of those who trained their cameras or pens on Amlasole or distributed 'relief ' to the people, did not attempt to explore the causes underlying the predicament of the people of the area. (Sinha, 2013:43).

The deaths of Lodha/Sabar individuals owing to hunger and malnutrition in Amlasole in Binpur II in Paschim (West) Medinipur raised a furor in West

---

[3] In 1977 the Left Front won the state assembly elections and the state was ruled by communists and other left groups till 2011.The Government formed by the coalition of leftist political parties in West Bengal is known as the Left Front Government. (LFG).The erstwhile left front led West Bengal state government holds the Indian record for the longest period of governance. Until 3 November, 2000, Jyoti Basu was the Chief Minister of the state. After his resignation, due to health reasons, Buddhadev Bhattacharya became the Chief Minister of West Bengal, who continued in office until 13 May, 2011. (Wikipedia accessed through Google on 17.10.2014).

Bengal few years back. The then Chief Minister of West Bengal had to order an inquiry by the government officials and it revealed the wretched living condition of this marginalized scheduled tribe of West Bengal. The episode also revealed another important fact. The Chief Minister himself stated in the media that there are many villages like Amlasole in the region and we have to take step towards the overall development of the area. This region later turned into a battlefield and according to media and police reports the Maoist groups formed their stronghold in this locale. Intellectuals and celebrities from Kolkata have visited this region and declared that the utter lack of development is the main cause of people's wrath against the Government and ruling party functionaries in this part of the district.

The two incidents narrated above are not isolated. They have a history. The history is the story of exploitation, marginalization, human right s violation, social exclusion and policy failures on the part of the Government to deliver social and economic justice to a group of voiceless people who were categorized by the colonial Government as 'Criminal Tribe' and then by the Independent Government as 'Denotified' and 'Primitive Tribal Group'. Does 'social harmony ' and 'inclusive development' bear significant meaning without the inclusion of this ethnic minority in the mainstream of a democratic country? Before we address this question, one should travel in space and time about the Lodha -Sabars. Who are they? How do they live and survive? Virtually, no recent empirical study exist on the survival strategies of this most marginalized community of the state, let alone concrete plans for their overall improvement in terms of socio-economic development. Surely, the Lodhas of West Bengal is one such community which has a long history of marginalization and oppression by the state and the dominant communities and they also have a history of demarginalization which had started in the post colonial period by the efforts of the state and non-state actors as well as the members of the community themselves.

In this book an attempt has been made to look into the twin process of marginalization vis-à-vis demarginalization of the Lodhas who are listed as a scheduled tribe[4] in India. The following chapters of the book deal with the

[4] In academics the word 'tribe' is used in anthropology as a conceptual category which refers to both as a 'type of society ' (simple, egalitarian) and a 'stage' (devoid of centralized authority which preceded states and kingdoms) in social evolution. (Sahlins, 1968). In the Indian context, the anthropologists distinguished tribes and at the same time related them with the caste society in a continuum. (Béteille, 1986 and Sinha, 1958). 'Tribe' in India is also treated as an administrative category for the purpose of positive discrimination (e.g., reservation in jobs). Recently, the tribes in India have also been viewed as 'indigenous peoples ' or 'adivasis' by the activists and social workers although the administrative

story of marginalization of the tribe in an historical frame of reference while at the same time we also provide a synchronic narrative of the process of demarginalization of the community based on our anthropological fieldwork and observations.

THE STORY OF MARGINALIZATION OF THE LODHAS IN AN HISTORICAL CONTEXT

Criminal Tribes in Colonial India

The Criminal Tribes Act dates back to successive pieces of legislation enforced in India during British rule. The legislation was first enacted in 1871 as the Criminal Tribes Act, 1871 which applied mostly in North India. The Act was extended to Bengal Presidency and other areas in 1876, and, finally, with the Criminal Tribes Act, 1911, it was extended to Madras Presidency as well. The Act went through several amendments in the next decade and, lastly, the Criminal Tribes Act, 1924 was enacted incorporating all the aforementioned provinces.(http://en.wikipedia.org/wiki/Criminal_Tribes_Act). Interestingly, in an article entitled 'The Criminal Tribes of India' published in the *Journal of the Royal Society of Arts* in 1923, a retired British administrative officer Frederick de L. Booth Tucker wrote:

> Crime in most countries is committed by individuals, in India usually by tribes, communities and gangs, who are highly organised and trained in it from childhood as a profession. The entire family and the relatives of an Indian criminal, including the women and children, are usually associated with him in the commission of crime. It is looked upon by these tribes very much as we regard the military profession, and is considered to be both honourable and lucrative. (Tucker, 1923:158-168).

According to Tucker, there were 18 settlements of criminal tribes and in the then Bengal Presidency there was only one such settlement and the community which was recorded by him as criminal was not the Lodhas but 'Karwal Nats'. Moreover, he stated in the same article that most of the families in those settlements were found to practice agriculture combined with

category still seems to be important even to the tribes themselves.(Xaxa, 1999a & 1999b). Lodhas are also classified as a scheduled tribe in India by the Government.

petty commodity production and the rest were engaged in industrial occupations. (Ibid). Tucker's description does not fit to the traditional occupation of the Lodhas practicing hunting gathering as was reported by the anthropologists much later. The question is how the Lodhas were included under the 'Criminal Tribe' category and brought under the purview of the Criminal Tribes Act, 1911?

In the same volume of the journal published after five months, another British official of the Police in his correspondence in connection with a remark made by Sir Edward Henry in the discussion on Commissioner Booth Tucker's paper dealing with Criminal Tribes Act observed:

> The chief motive of the Act is to save criminal tribes from themselves; to reform and to reclaim them, so far as is humanly possible. The Act, as it stands, supplies to the criminal classes a method by which they may be able to improve themselves and to lead decent lives. To the general public it affords a scheme of protection while it places at the disposal of the police a lawful means for keeping potential criminals under proper supervision (Faulkner, 1923:449).

Faulkner in the conclusion of his correspondence mentioned how the Lodhas of the then Bengal Presidency might have been designated as a Criminal Tribe by the local administration who were empowered by the law to declare a whole tribe as criminal if a section of the community were found to commit certain non-bailable offences. We should quote Faulkner verbatim:

> If only a part of the tribe is addicted to the systematic commission of non-bailable offences, then only that part of the tribe may be declared a criminal tribe for the purposes of the Act. This was, to my knowledge, done in the case of certain gangs of the tribe of Lodhas in the district of Midnapur(Ibid).

The above exchange between the two experienced British officials revealed the truth that the Lodhas as a community were not initially included under the designation of a criminal tribe at least like the other communities of India but some members of the community were definitely declared as 'Criminal' as early as the first half of 20th Century and then by the immense scope of the law and the discretion of the British officials the whole community was classified as a Criminal Tribe. Be that as it may, one thing was clear in the basic premise of the Criminal Tribe Act. The premise was clearly explicated in the first quote from Booth Tucker 's article wherein he opined that crime in India was committed by *'tribes, communities and gangs '* who were *'trained in it from childhood as a profession'* and they regarded crimes *'to be both honourable and lucrative'* profession like the westerners who viewed military profession as admirable. (Authors' emphasis).

From Criminal to Denotified Tribe: The Post Colonial Story

After the Independence, a number of communities in India who were designated as 'Criminal Tribes' by the British colonial administration were redesignated as 'Denotified tribe s' and later some of them have been classified as 'Primitive Tribal Groups' (PTG). (Verma, 1990).The Lodha of West Bengal is one of them, who suffered from continued poverty and marginalization (Devi, 1983). In 1952, the Criminal Tribes Act was repealed by the Government of India and all the communities who were designated as criminal tribes were reclassified as denotified communities. Once again, in the name of 'positive discrimination ' they were reclassified into another governmental category without being given equal status with the mainstream communities of the nation. Furthermore, the denotification process also carried the colonial hangover of looking at those 'Criminal Tribes' as born criminals. G.N. Devi, a noted scholar-activist and the editor of *Budhan, the newsletter of the Denotified Nomadic Tribes Rights Action Groups (DNT-RAG)* narrated the passage from the Criminal Tribes Act of the colonial period to the post colonial Denotified Tribes Act in a succinct manner.

> Soon after Independence, the communities notified as criminal tribals were denotified by the Government. This notification was followed by substitution of a series of Acts, generally entitled 'Habitual Offenders Act'. The HOAs preserved most of the provisions of the former CT Acts, except the premise implicit in it that an entire community can be 'born' criminal. Apparently, the denotification and the passing of the HOAs should have ended the misery of the communities penalised under the CT Act. But that has not happened. The police forces as well as the people in general were taught to look upon the 'Criminal Tribes' as born criminals during the colonial times. That attitude continues to persist even today. (Devi, 1998).

In the post-Independence period the 'Ex-criminal' and 'Denotified' Lodhas also suffered extreme humiliation and human right s violation not only from the higher Hindu castes but also from the Santals, the dominant tribe of the region. The anthropologist, Probodh Bhowmick in one of his articles narrated how the Lodhas in the bank of river Subarnarekha in erstwhile Midnapore district were chased and finally thirty-nine of them were brutally beheaded and the rest were taken to the custody of the killers in September 1979. (Bhowmick, 1981:6).In the same article Bhowmick reported that in an earlier incident in 1968 the houses of eighteen Lodha villages were burned by the Santals (Ibid, 1981:6). The famous litterateur and social activist Mahasweta Devi reported in her 1983 article published in *Economic and Political Weekly*, 'Lodha killing is a regular feature in West Bengal ' and she enumerated the killing of thirty four Lodhas in West Bengal from 1979-1982. (Devi, 1983:947).

Under this post-colonial scenario, various welfare measures have been undertaken by the Central Government to improve the living conditions of the Lodhas. After the independence of India many plans and projects of specific nature have been initiated by the Government to resettle the forest dependent and semi-nomadic Lodha minority community in an agriculture dependent sedentary life. Meanwhile, a good number of rehabilitation schemes have been formulated and implemented on the Lodhas and most of these schemes failed and no lasting impact of them could be made. (Bhowmick, 1985:17). In the post-Independence period the main aim of the Government was to put off the stigma of criminal tribe designation of the Lodhas. At the same time the Government also wanted to uplift the socio-economic condition of this tribe who mainly depended on forest produce and daily labour. After the sixties, the Lodhas were included under the Denotified and nomadic tribes along with 19 communities of West Bengal (https://www.indianfolklore.org/journals/index.php/Mukt/.../134 2012).

The Central Government had taken special initiatives for improving the living condition of the Lodhas by providing facilities for housing, agriculture, cottage industries and education through Ashram Hostel from the primary level (Bhowmick, 1985:15). But the traditional life of the Lodhas has not changed much. Still they are dependent on forest produce collection and hunting some jungle animal for livelihood. (Bhowmick, 1963:26).

In the recent period some members of the minority ethnic group, that is Lodha/Kheria/Sabar however got themselves educated and began to enter the modern institutions located in the urban and semi-urban areas of West Bengal. But even within the modern institutions they were found to be marginalized and faced discriminations of various kinds. A notable example is the case of the first Lodha graduate named Chuni Kotal [5] who was a girl hailing from a very poor and uneducated Lodha family in Paschim Medinipur district of West Bengal. Chuni committed suicide on 16th August, 1992 in Medinipur. She was a student of the Anthropology Department of Vidyasagar University. She alleged that a teacher of the Anthropology Department belonging to the majority community (a high caste Brahmin) used to harass and insult her by mentioning her low origin. The West Bengal Government constituted a one man enquiry committee by a retired judge of the Calcutta High Court which acquitted the teacher. (*Report of the Ganguly Commission of Enquiry,* 1992). The suicide of Chuni created a lot of hue and cry in the media and the political circles which resonated time and again in the academic literature (Chanda, 2005: 130-141; Devi, 1992: 1836-1837).

[5] According to Wikipedia 'Chuni Kotal was born in 1965, in village Gohaldohi, in present Paschim Medinipur district, West Bengal, in a poor Lodha family. Chuni Kotal survived a childhood of impoverishment to become the first woman from a 'primitive' tribe to complete High School. Thereafter, she got her first job as a Lodha social worker in 1983 at Jhargram ITDP office, surveying local villages. Eventually she graduated in anthropology from Vidyasagar University, in 1985. Two years after graduating, she was appointed as a Hostel superintendent at 'Rani Shiromoni Scheduled Caste and Scheduled Tribe Girls' Hostel at Medinipur, here again she had to face the social stigma attached with her tribe. Trouble really began for her when she joined the Master's course (M.Sc.) at the local Vidyasagar University. Here she was continuously discriminated against and insulted by her upper caste Brahmin professors (like Professor Falguni Chakraborty and others) and university administrators, who refused to give her the requisite pass grades, despite her having fulfilled the criteria, who opined that a low-born person coming from a "criminal tribe", now a Denotified tribe of India, hence did not have the social privilege and pre-ordained destiny to study "higher discourse" like the social sciences. In 1991, after losing two years at the course, she complained, and a high level enquiry commission was set up by the state Education minister to no avail, once the fact that she belonged to a former criminal tribe came to light. Wikipedia further informed that on 14 August 1992, frustrated by years of casteist and racist harassment at Medinipur, she left Medinipur and went to meet her husband, Manmatha Savar, who had been working at Railway workshop at Kharagpur. They had known each other since 1981 and later married in 1990 through a court marriage ; Manmatha was a high school graduate himself. It was here that she committed suicide on August 16, 1992, at the age of 27. Her death became the focal point of immense political, human right s and social controversy in the media in West Bengal, and eastern India where the discourse is traditionally Brahmin-Baniya dominated. However, her death did not receive the attention of Indian American social science professors as it did among Western social scientists who were studying the Indian caste system, like Professor Nicholas B. Dirks at Columbia University and Professor Jan Breman at the University of Amsterdam. (http://en.wikipedia.org/wiki/Chuni_Kotal accessed through Google on 22.10.2014).

Still later, since 1971, the Lodhas were redesignated as one of the 'Primitive Tribal Groups'[6] (PTGs) of India, another governmental category. (Verma, 1990: 277). Special funds have been sanctioned by the Government to organize a Development Cell under the Project Officer and Backward Class Welfare Officer (PO and BCW) of the state Government. (Bhowmick, 1985: 14).

Through the Cell (PO and BCW) of Government has delivered various types of development inputs for strengthening of the socio-economic condition of this marginalized community. Another important component of the governmental perspective centering round the development of the Lodhas was to settle this tribe as an agriculturist population.

The *District Human Development Report: Paschim Medinipur* (DHDR) published by the Government of West Bengal in 2011 devoted a long section on the Lodhas in which we find a good description of the poor socio-economic condition of the tribe in a historical perspective. The report concluded that even after Independence the marginalized condition of the Lodhas in Paschim Medinipur and other adjoining places have not improved appreciably. The report revealed that the Government regarded the Lodhas as a kind of primitive and displaced group of people who needed rehabilitation within the fold of an agricultural economy. In the report it was admitted that the governmental efforts towards the development of the tribe largely failed. To quote

> … the Government came forward to do welfare work in the form of house construction, goat-rearing etc. But all these efforts ended in a fiasco and became the butt of criticism. Then, these groups of people were treated as Primitive Tribal Groups(1979) when special assistance was given and Lodha cell under the I.T.D.P. was constituted for utilizing funds profitably through the blocks, headed by a project officer located at Jhargram (*District Human Development Report: Paschim Medinipu,* 2011:234*)*. The DHDR however did not contain any description or assessment on the utilization of the development assistance given to the Lodhas of Paschim Medinipur district.

[6] The criteria of inclusion of a tribal community under Primitive Tribal Group (PTG) are: i) Pre-agricultural level of technology, ii) very low level of literacy, iii) declining or stagnant population and iv) a subsistence level of economy. (Meena, 2009:13)

Chapter II

ANTHROPOLOGISTS AND ACTIVISTS VIEW LODHAS: THE SECOND PART OF THE POST COLONIAL STORY

OVERVIEW

The Lodhas are now treated as one of the denotified communities by the Central Government. In West Bengal, Lodhas are mainly concentrated in the districts of Paschim (West) Medinipur and Purba (East) Medinipur. As mentioned earlier, in the pre-Independence period they were treated as a Criminal Tribe till the revocation of the Criminal Tribes Act in 1952. In the first Census of India after Independence the Lodhas were recorded as a scheduled caste and their total population was returned to be 8,346 only in West Bengal (Mitra 1953:89). According to the Census of 1951 the Lodhas were found to be distributed in the districts of Burdwan, Birbhum, Bankura, Midnapore, Hooghly, Howrah, 24 Parganas, Calcutta, Murshidabad and Jalpaiguri. In 1951, they were not found in the North Bengal districts like Nadia, Maldah, West Dinajpur, Darjeeling and Cooch Behar. In the same Census the total number of Lodhas in erstwhile Midnapore was 7040, that is 84.35 percent of the then total population of Lodhas in West Bengal. (Ibid:89-90).

The Census of 1981 showed that the total population of the Lodhas including the Kharias and the Kherias of West Bengal was 53,718. The Lodhas were concentrated in Midnapore District and their total number according to the Census of 1981 was 16,534. Besides West Bengal, they were also found in the Mayurbhanj and Baleswar districts of Orissa, Originally, they inhabited hilly rugged terrains covered with jungle. Their mother tongue is Lodha, which is close to Savara, an Austro-Asiatic language. They are fluent in Bengali. Traditionally, they were forest dwellers but now they have started cultivation either as owner or as agricultural labourer and are also engaged in hunting and fishing. More than 80% of them follow Hinduism with traditional belief in spirits and nature (Mandal, H. et al. 2002:32).

At present the Lodhas do not live exclusively in the forest covered areas, but have spread out in other deforested regions and are found to work there as agricultural and non-agricultural labourers. But their main economy is still based on collection of minor forest products, such as leaves for preparing leaf-plates for sale. According to Bhowmick, the Lodhas were found to collect edible roots and fruits for household consumption and sell the surplus in the local markets. They are also found to be engaged in the collection of tussore cocoons (*vide* glossary for the meaning of the term) and sell them in the market for cash. Lodhas also catch snakes and lizards and sell their hides and consume the flesh of these animals. They also catch fish and tortoises from the water bodies for domestic consumption as well as for sale. (Bhowmick, 1981:6).

THE VIEWS OF THE ANTHROPOLOGISTS AND ACTIVISTS

One of the eminent anthropologists of India Probodh Kumar Bhowmick reported that various types of developmental initiatives had been undertaken by the Government and some non-governmental organizations to settle the Lodhas for leading a sedentary agricultural life. In 1950s a rehabilitation project was taken up on an experimental basis for the Lodha families at Daharpur of Narayangarh block in erstwhile Medinipur district. This project included development inputs like house building, land purchase, land recovery, supply of domestic and agricultural training to be imparted to the Lodhas for their resettlement. But this developmental programme could not be implemented in the aforesaid area owing to some serious difference of opinion among the organisers and social scientists associated with that project (Bhowmick, 1981:7).

According to another eminent Indian anthropologist Ajit Kumar Danda, the Lodhas belong to Mundari speaking population who are mostly found in the forest covered areas of Singhbhum District of Jharkhand, Mayurbhanj District of Odisha (formerly known as Orissa) and Midnapore District of West Bengal, which is also known as Jungle Mahal since in the colonial period they were found to inhabit mainly in the three aforementioned states of India. They speak a dialect composed of distorted Bengali, Oriya and words of Mundari origin. (Danda, 2002:103)

The Government of Independent India repealed the Criminal Tribes Act in 1952. Even after denotification as criminal tribes, the Lodhas continue to suffer from the social stigma and the non-tribal neighbours still behave unsympathetically towards them. Over the decades, the Lodhas gradually changed their occupation from hunting gathering to agriculture as an alternative means of livelihood owing to deforestation. (Danda, 2002:110-111).

On the activist side, one of the most important observers of the marginalized condition of the Lodhas in West Bengal is Mahasweta Devi. She not only wrote on the abject poverty and exploitation of the Lodhas, but also worked for decades to fulfill the various demands of the community as regards their socio-economic condition. Although, not an anthropologist, Mahasweta Devi has firsthand personal experiences of the failures of governmental schemes and shortcomings of the government policies directed towards the development of the Lodhas in erstwhile Midnapore, and the adjoining districts of West Bengal. Unlike academic anthropologists, she practiced activism through the publication of a Bengali literary magazine (*Bartika*) in which many literate tribal persons including Lodhas wrote about their living conditions, violence committed to them by the state and higher classes of the society and the demands of the different tribal communities. The autobiography of Chuni Kotal was published first in Bartika magazine in November 1982 which revealed extreme poverty among the Lodha families in the state of West Bengal (https://www.academia.edu/7214762/Atmakatha_by_Chuni_Kotal).

Mahasveta Devi herself also wrote a number of articles in Bengali and English in which she depicted the ground realities regarding the problems of the implementation of development inputs and schemes among the Lodhas. In one of her articles published in the *Economic and Political Weekly* in 1983, Mahasveta Devi cited examples of some Lodha villages in the present Paschim Medinipur district in which Government schemes have failed to reach the beneficiaries, although they were badly in need of the development programmes. In the article Mahasweta Devi categorically pointed out

> Usually the schemes are made by people not knowing or caring to know what the tribal really need. The plan is then, after the usual procedures, left to the contractor.... I have seen contractor-made

> construction works meant for the Lodhas. It is better to make specious earthen huts. With a structure of cement, brick and sand, the inevitable contractor is bound to enter the scene. To whose benefit? Not the Lodhas'. Over three decades, huge sums have been spent in the name of the Lodhas and the community has gone much below the poverty line s. (Devi, 1983:948).

Mahasweta Devi's long experience of working actively for the cause of the Lodhas led her to advocate certain concrete solutions which she thought should have been adopted by the policy makers and Government functionaries for the development of this small and marginalized community of Bengal. According to her, plans with big budgets plans may not work for the real development of the Lodhas and secondly, development inputs for the community should be executed and managed by the Lodhas themselves. In another article published in the *Economic and Political Weekly*, Mahasweta Devi narrated her experience of observing the enthusiasm created among the Lodhas when in 1982-83, they revived their own community organization (*Lodha -Sabar Kalayan Samiti*). We quote:

> The Lodhas had revived the Samiti in sheer desperation for physical survival. The awakening of the Lodhas surprised the state government. The sluggish serpent eternally in winter hibernation covering the Lodha name seemed to stir a little. Six Lodhas were appointed as Lodha cell social workers, including Chuni Kotal. And three boys were appointed as village welfare supervisors in Chakua, Chandabila and Pranabpalli, on contingency basis, at ten rupees a day. All were employed in September 1983. .... This encouraged the Lodhas, through their devotion and dedication Lodha and some non-Lodha children came to the community centre for studying. These workers could persuade the Lodhas to give up drinking, to save from their wages, to live hygienically. They felt that the state government was coming forward with schemes for development and the Lodhas should be prepared to reap the full benefit of such schemes (Devi, 1985:1467).

Various types of development schemes have been implemented among the Lodhas since Independence. In 1954, both West Bengal and the Central Government s jointly made attempts to improve the economic condition of a group of fifty Lodha families at Alugeria under the police station of Jhargram in erstwhile Medinipur district through the Bengal Branch of the Gandhite *Harijan Sabak Sangha*, a voluntary organization. A sum of Rs. 1500/- per family was allotted under various heads of expenditure, such as house purchase, purchase of bullocks, goats and agricultural implements. After some period, this scheme had failed for lack of proper planning and execution. Later, the state Government entrusted the work to the *Bharat Savashram Sangha* another all-India voluntary organization, who undertook a rehabilitation scheme at Dholkat village under the police station of Jhargram. The Sangha authorities selected a site near their center and constructed twenty five residential huts with corrugated asbestos and tin sheet roofs (Narayan, 1988:44-45).

In the 1960s the state Government had entrusted another voluntary organization named *Samaj Sebak Sangha* with the work of organizing a colony of the Lodhas in Narayangarh in present Paschim (West) Medinipur district. Anthropologists and social workers under the leadership of Probodh Kumar Bhowmick were involved in this task. Altogether, thirty nine families (on an average expenditure of Rs. 1500/- per family) were resettled at Daharpur under the police station of Narayangarh (Ibid:45).

A Multi-Purpose Cooperative society as per direction of the Tribal Welfare Department of the Government of West Bengal distributed land on family basis to settle the Lodhas as agriculturists. The Central and State Governments allocated a good number of tiled residential huts, bullocks and goats to these Lodha families. (Ibid:46).

Mr. Nalini Bera, a Government official has written an excellent Bengali novel on the life of the Lodhas which was dedicated to Chuni Kotal. The name of the novel is *Sabar Charit* (2005) which literally means 'The nature of the Sabar'. In the novel, which is based on the personal experiences of the author, the daily lives of some Lodha women are depicted in painstaking detail. The characters in the novel were mainly found to eke out their living through the collection of various forest products (Bera, 2005).The author, in a literary vein, however did not deal with the problems of implementation of the development schemes as narrated by Mahasweta Devi in her articles.

Chapter III

The Study Area and the People

The State of West Bengal

West Bengal is a state in the eastern region of India and is the fourth-most populous state of the nation with over 91 million inhabitants. Spread over 34,267 sq mi (88,750 km^2), it is bordered by Bangladesh, Nepal and Bhutan, and the Indian states Odisha, Jharkhand, Bihar, Sikkim, and Assam. The state capital is Kolkata. Together with the neighboring nation of Bangladesh and parts of the state of Tripura, it makes up the ethno-linguistic region of Bengal. According to the provisional results of the 2011 national census, West Bengal is the fourth most populous state in India with a population of 91,347,736 (7.55% of India's population). Bengalees comprise the majority of the population. West Bengal is home to a number of indigenous tribal communities such as Santal, Munda, Lodha Kol, and Toto tribes. At present there are 40 scheduled tribes in West Bengal. According to the last Census of 2011 the total tribal population in the state is 52, 96,953 and the Lodha/Kharia/Kheria are 1, 08,707. (*Tribal Health Bulletin*, 2014.)

Ancient Bengal was the site of several major Vedic kingdoms. It was part of large Indian empires such as the Maurya Empire (second century BC) and Gupta Empire (fourth century AD); and part of the regional Pala Empire (eighth to 11th century) and Sena dynasty (11th–12th centuries). From the 13th century onward, the region was ruled by several Sultans, Hindu kings and Baro-Bhuyan landlords, until the beginning of British rule in the 18th century. The British East India Company established their rule in the region following the Battle of Plassey in 1757, and Calcutta served for many years as the capital of British India. The early and prolonged exposure to British administration resulted in expansion of Western education, culminating in development in science, institutional education, and social reforms of the region, including what became known as the Bengal Renaissance. A hotbed of the Indian Independence movement through the early 20th century, Bengal was divided during India's independence in 1947 along religious lines into two separate entities: West Bengal —a state of India—and East Bengal—a part of the newly created Pakistani Dominion—later becoming the independent nation of Bangladesh in 1971. West Bengal is a major agricultural producer, the sixth-largest contributor to India's net domestic product. Well-known for its political activism, the state was ruled by democratically elected communist government for 34 years, starting from 1977. It is notable for its cultural activities and presence of cultural and educational institutions; the state capital Kolkata is known as the "cultural capital of India". The state's cultural heritage, besides varied folk traditions, ranges from stalwarts in literature including Nobel-laureate Rabindranath Tagore to scores of musicians, film-makers and artists. (Wikipedia accessed on 17.10.2014 through Google).

Government and Politics

West Bengal is governed through a parliamentary system of representative democracy, a feature the state shares with other Indian states. Universal suffrage is granted to residents. There are two branches of Government. The legislature, the West Bengal Legislative Assembly, consists of elected members and special office bearers such as the Speaker and Deputy Speaker that are elected by the members. Assembly meetings are presided over by the Speaker or the Deputy Speaker in the Speaker's absence. The judiciary is composed of the Calcutta High Court and a system of lower courts. Executive authority is vested in the Council of Ministers headed by the Chief Minister, although the titular head of Government is the Governor. The Governor is the head of state appointed by the President of India. The leader of the party or coalition with a majority in the Legislative Assembly is appointed as the Chief Minister by the Governor and the Council of Ministers are appointed by the Governor on the advice of the Chief Minister.

The Council of Ministers reports to the Legislative Assembly. The Assembly is unicameral with 295 Members of the Legislative Assembly, or MLAs, including one nominated from the Anglo-Indian community. Terms of office run for 5 years, unless the Assembly is dissolved prior to the completion of the term.

Auxiliary authorities known as *panchayats*, for which local body elections are regularly held, govern local affairs. The state contributes 42 seats to Lok Sabha and 16 seats to Rajya Sabha of the Indian Parliament. (Ibid).

Brief Description of the District Paschim (West) Medinipur

The undivided Medinipur was the largest district (22°57'10" N to 21°36'35" N & 88°12'40" E to 86°33'50"E) in West Bengal and according to the Census 1991, covered an area of 9786.00 sq. km. with a total population of 83, 49,890. Medinipur has chequered annals since ancient times. The district was named after the author of a book Medinikosha. The Chinese traveler Fa-hien and Huen Tsang visited the riverine part Tamralipta (modern Tamluk) that rose to the pinnacle of prosperity during the 5th-7th century AD in 1783. Medinipur town became the Headquarters of the district Medinipur which became famous during the struggle of Independence against the British Raj. The district had 7 sub-divisions, 46 police stations, 54 development blocks, a zilla parishad (the highest tier of the elected local self-government) and 518 gram panchayats (the lowest tier of the elected local self-government). On 1st January 2002, the district was divided into two parts Paschim (West) Medinipur and Purba (East) Medinipur.

Paschim Medinipur district is situated in South-Western side of West Bengal. It is bounded by Bankura and Purulia districts in the north; Mayurbhanj and Balasore district of Orissa in the south; Hooghly and Purba Medinipur district in the east and Singbhum district of Jharkhand and Purulia district of West Bengal in the west.

The Paschim Medinipur district is divided into 4 subdivisions, which are: (i) Jhargram (ii) Sadar Subdivision, (iii) Kharagpur, and (iv) Ghatal. According to the Census of 2001, there were 7581 villages and 8701 *mouzas* (the smallest revenue collection unit in India) under the district. It has 29 Blocks, 290 Gram Panchayat s and 3491 Gram Samsads (District Statistical Handbook 2006:4).

Topographically, the district can broadly be divided into three parts.

a) Almost entirely flat plain in the east.
b) Undulating extensions of Chhotanagpur plateau on the west.

c) The Kanthi coastal plain on the south. Major rivers of the district are Rupnarayan, Kangsabati, Subarnarekha, Haldi, and Kaliag etc. The district gradually slopes from the Chhotonagpur plateau to the 'Kanthi littoral plain' bordering the Bay of Bengal.

d)

WEST BENGAL

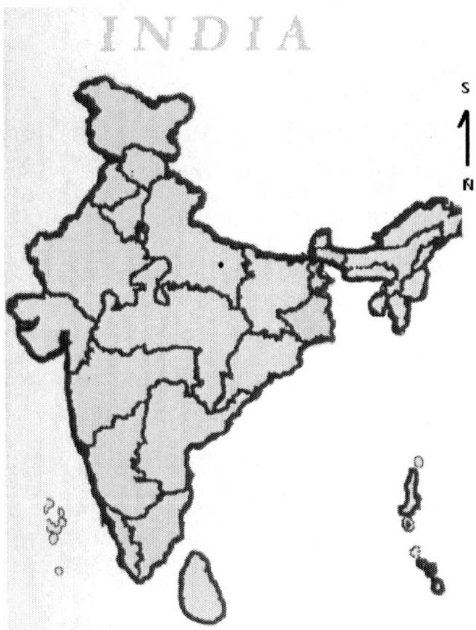

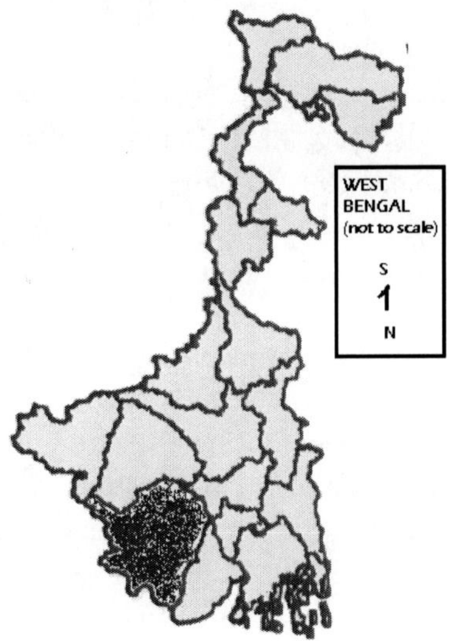

Vast expanse of land of the district is composed of alluvial saline and saline alkali, older alluvia, sandy and gravelly soils and saline alkali is found along the narrow littoral part of the district.

The climate is tropical. Normal rainfall is 1560mm. and average rainfall of the district is 1537 mm. The climate is characterised by hot summer, cold winter, abundant rainfall and humidity from 1450mm to 1560mm per year. (District Statistical Handbook 2006:1)

More than 64% of the total land is cultivable and 28% is irrigated. The irrigation projects of the district are 'High Level Medinipur Canal' and 'Kangsabati Reservoir Project'. The district is predominantly agricultural. Rice is the main crop and jute, potato, til (an oilseed), linseed and vegetables are grown all over the district. The cashew-nut growing areas are Kanthi, Garbeta and Jhargram.

PASCHIM MEDINIPUR

Western part of the district is covered with forest (13%) where trees like *Sal* (*Shorea robusta*), *Mohua(Madhuca longifolia*), *Palas(Butea monosperma*), *Neem(Azadirachta indica*), are grown abundantly. Floriculture is the mainstay of the people of Mecheda, Bhogpur and Panskura. Pisciculture is the main occupation in the coastal areas.

About 89.90% population of Paschim Medinipur district lives in the rural area, whereas, 19 urban centers support 10.1% of the population. Kharagpur, having the biggest Railway workshop of South-Eastern Railway, Indian Institute of Technology and other socio-cultural centers are the major urban agglomerations of the district. Haldia is the most important modern port and petrochemical industrial complex. Medinipur is famous for its handcrafts and small-scale industries. Kolkata/Bombay National Highway (NH-6) and Southeastern Railway pass through the heart of the district. With the available resources and potentialities, Medinipur has a bright future of agro-industrial development and planning.

The district has a population of 59, 13,457 according to Census 2011 [males 3,007,885 (50.86%) and females 2,905,572 (49.14%)]. Population density of the district is 631 persons per square km. Sex ratio is 966 females per 1000 males. The Census 2011 reported total scheduled tribe population was 880,015.

According to District Statistical Handbook 2006, there are 4671 Primary school s, 136 Middle schools, 384 High schools, 243 Higher Secondary schools, 18 general colleges and one University (Vidyasagar University) in the district. According to the Census of 2001, seventy percent of the total population of the Paschim Medinipur district was found to be literate.

The Demographic Figures of the Rural Areas of the District

According to the 2011 census, 87.78 % population of Paschim Medinipur districts lives in rural areas of villages. The total population of Paschim Medinipur district living in rural areas is 5,190,771 of which males and females are 2,641,721 and 2,549,050 respectively. In rural areas of Paschim Medinipur district, sex ratio is 965 females per 1000 males. If child sex ratio data of Paschim Medinipur district is considered, the figure is 962 girls per 1000 boys. Child population in the age 0-6 is 616,836 in rural areas of which males are 314,452 and there are 302,384 females. The child population comprises 11.90 % of total rural population of Paschim Medinipur district. Literacy rate in rural areas of Paschim Medinipur district is 76.87 % as per census data 2011. Gender wise, male and female literacy stood at 84.52 and 68.94 percent respectively. In total, 3,515,817 people were literate of which males and females were 1,967,008 and 1,548,809 respectively. (http://www.census2011.co.in/census/district/18-paschim-medinipur.html).

Brief description of the Jhargram Subdivision

Total population – 1,008,030 (Census 2001)
Scheduled caste population - 185,484 (Census 2001)
Scheduled Tribe population – 302,588 (Census 2001).

Jhargram is located at 22.45° N 86.98° E. It has an average elevation of 81 meters (265 feet). The Jhargram subdivision of Paschim Medinipur district in West Bengal is mainly a forest-covered area and the majority of the people belong to various scheduled tribes, viz. Santal, Munda, Lodha, Kora and Bhumij. This subdivision belongs to rainfed area. The average annual rainfall in this subdivision is 1463 mm. Forest resource collection, daily wage labour, seasonal migration and agricultural work are the main means of livelihood of the poor in this area. It consists of Jhargram municipality and eight community development blocks, which are Binpur I, Binpur II, Jamboni, Jhargram, Gopiballavpur I, Gopiballavpur II, Nayagram and Sankrail. The eight blocks contain 79 gram panchayats. The subdivision has its headquarters at Jhargram. There is no urban area under these eight blocks. Beyond the Gangetic plains of Bengal, Jhargram offers the most exotic beauties of undulating topography culminating in hill ranges of Belpahari, Kankrajhor in the North to the peaceful beauties of meandering Subarnarekha River in the South. Jhargram is the paradise of nature lovers with abundant forests of Sal and Mahua trees as well as wild fauna like elephant, deer and a variety of birds. The ancient temples, royal palaces, folk tunes and rhythms of tribal dance and music make it all the more attractive destination of tourists who love to discover the unknown and unaffected beauties of nature.

BRIEF DESCRIPTION OF THE ADMINISTRATIVE BLOCKS IN THE STUDY AREA

BINPUR II

Total population: 145,977 (Census 2001) 130,053 (The population figures of the blocks as per Census of India 2011 were not available at the time of writing the book)

Schedule caste population: 21,388 (Census 2001)

Schedule Tribe population: 61,469 (Census 2001)

Human Development Index (HDI): 0.479

Binpur is a rural administrative block in Jhargram subdivision of Paschim Medinipur district

Binpur-II is located 22°35′00″N 86°54′55″E/22.833800°N86.9151760°E/ 22.5833800; 86.9151760. This block is covered by hilly and forest covered terrains.

Demographic Profile of Binpur II

According to the 2001 Census, Binpur II block had a population of 145,913 out of which 73,633 were males and 72,280 females. Decadal population growth for the period 1991-2001 was 13.86% for Binpur II, against 15.68% in (erstwhile) Medinipur district. Binpur II block had a population of 145,913 out of which 73,633 were males and 72,280 females. Decadal growth for the period 1991-2001 was 12.20% for Binpur II, against 15.68% in (erstwhile) Medinipur district. The decadal growth of population in West Bengal was 17.84% during the same period.

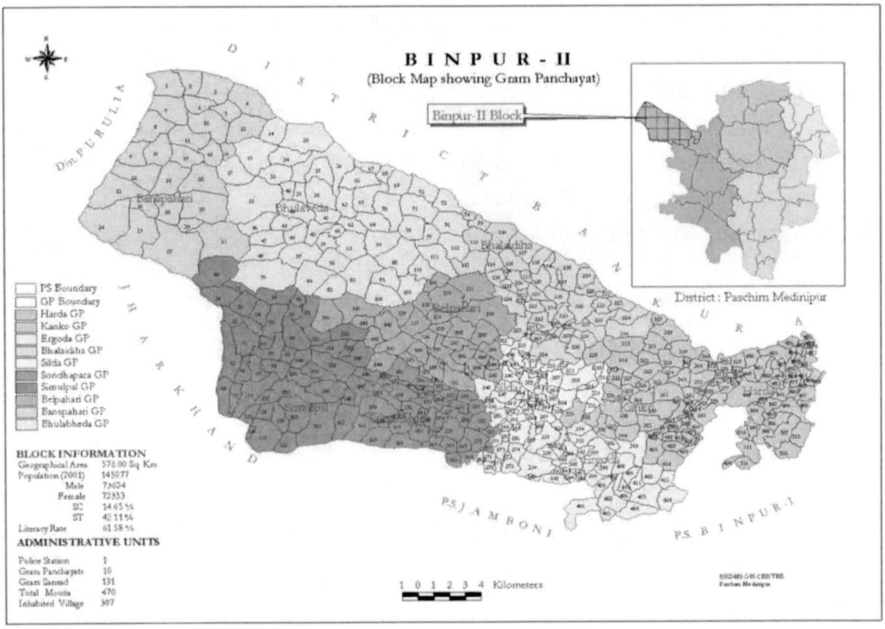

According to *District Human Development Report: Paschim Medinipur*, the human development index of Binpur II is very low and the rank is 27 from the top out of 29 blocks of Paschim Medinipur district. (DHDR. 2011: 17).

NAYAGRAM

Total population: 123,929 (Census 2001)

Scheduled caste population: 22,757 (Census 2001)

Scheduled Tribe population: 49,387(Census 2001)

Human Development Index (HDI): 0.423

Nayagram is a rural block and a Police station in Jhargram subdivision of Paschim Medinipur district. Nayagram is located at 22°02′N 87°11′E/22.03°N 87.18°E/22.03; 87.18 [1]. It has an average elevation of 15 meters (52 feet). Nayagram is situated on the bank of the Subarnarekha River.

According to 2001 census, Nayagram block had a population of 123,929 out of which 62,588 were males and 61,341 females. Decadal population growth for the period 1991-2001 was 16.38% for Nayagram as against 15.68% in (erstwhile) Medinipur district. In the same period the decadal growth of population in West Bengal was 17.84%.

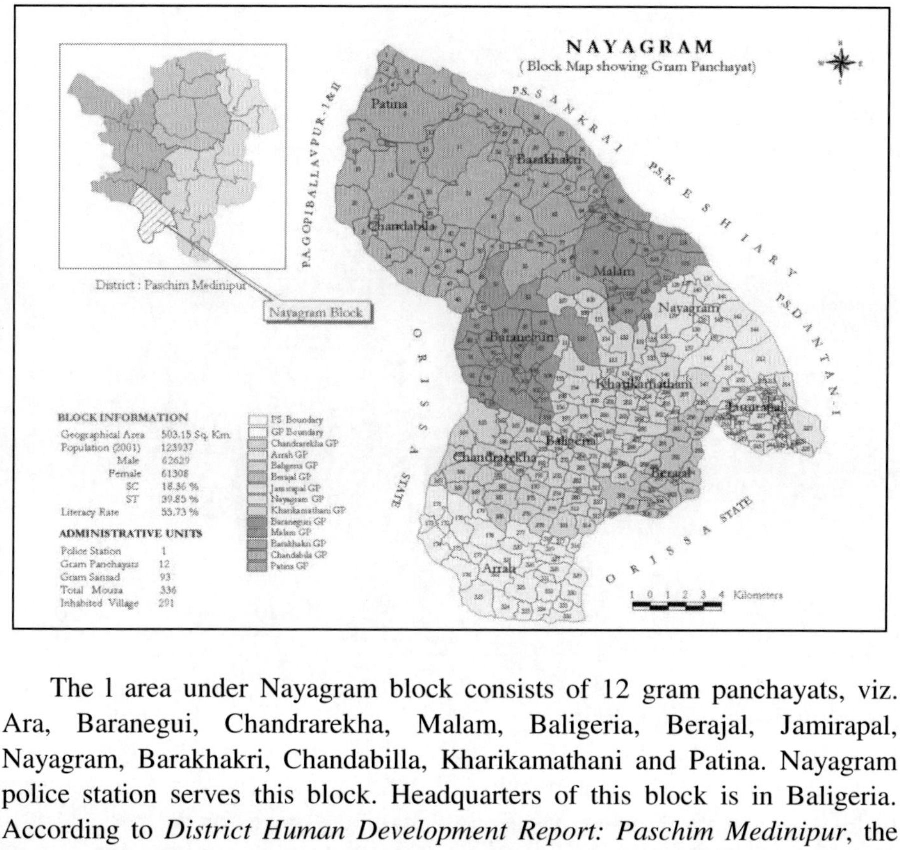

The 1 area under Nayagram block consists of 12 gram panchayats, viz. Ara, Baranegui, Chandrarekha, Malam, Baligeria, Berajal, Jamirapal, Nayagram, Barakhakri, Chandabilla, Kharikamathani and Patina. Nayagram police station serves this block. Headquarters of this block is in Baligeria. According to *District Human Development Report: Paschim Medinipur*, the human development index of Nayagram block is extremely poor since it comes last in terms of rank, which is 29 (DHDR. 2011:17).

NARAYANGARH

Total population: 266,675

Schedule Caste population: 48,443 (Census 2001)

Schedule Tribe population: 57,527 (Census 2001)

Human Development Index (HDI): 0.569

Naryangarh is a block in Kharagpur Subdivision of Paschim Medinipur District. Narayangarh block consists of 16 gram panchayats, viz. Bakhrabad, Hemchandra, Manya, Pakurseni, Belda I, Khursi, Mokrampur, Ranisarai, Belda II, Kunarpur, Narayangarh, Tutranga, Gramraj, Kushbasan, Narma and Kashipur. There is no urban area under this block.

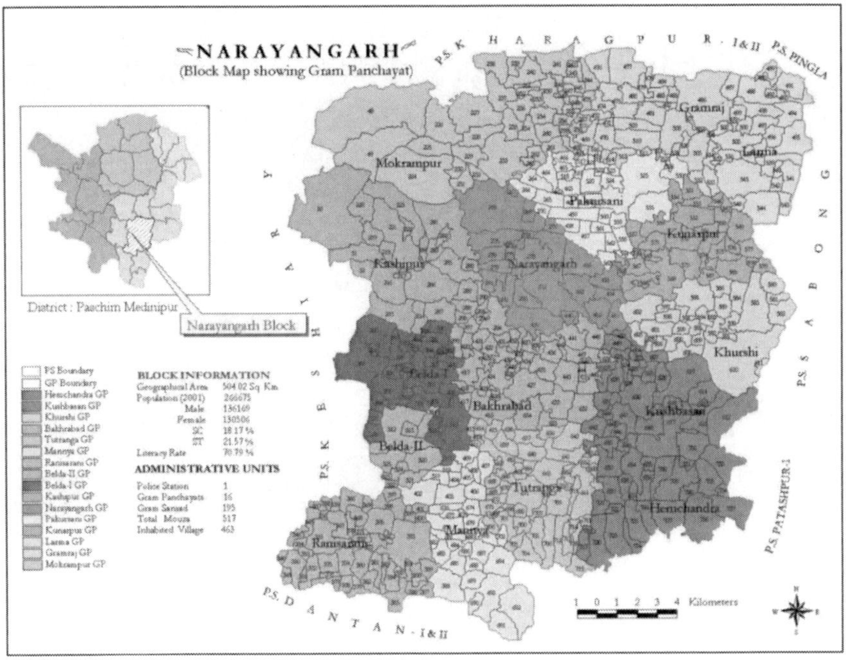

Natarayangarh and Belda police stations serve this block. Administrative Headquarters of this block is situated in Belda. According to 2001 census, Narayangarh block had a population of 266,675 out of which 136,169 were males and 130,506 females. Decadal population growth for the period 1991-2001 was 17.02% for Narayangarh, against 15.68% in (erstwhile) Medinipur district. Decadal population growth in West Bengal was 17.84% in the same period (District Statistical Handbook 2006:5). According to *District Human Development Report: Paschim Medinipur*, the human development index of Narayangarh block is lies in middle position among all the blocks of Paschim Medinipur (West) (DHDR. 2011:17).

Brief Description of the Villages in the Study Area

Daharpur (J.L No. 26)

Daharpur is a multi-caste village of Makarampur Gram Panchayat in Narayangar block of Paschim Medinipur district of West Bengal. The village is situated 1 km. from the National Highway 64; it is situated 15 km away from Midnapore town. The *mouza* name is also Daharpur. In this village there are two hamlets locally known as *paras*. One is *Uttar para*(North) in which live the Lodhas and the caste Hindu groups while the Paschim Para(West) is inhabited only by the Lodhas. Most of the villagers are engaged in cultivation as owner cultivators and agricultural labourers.

This village has two primary school s and Integrated Child Development Scheme (ICDS) centers within its boundary. Each hamlet (*para*) has a school and an ICDS centre. There is one High school at Bidisha which was established by the anthropologist Prof. P.K. Bhowmick. In this village, we have found six self-help-groups(SHGs) which are constituted by Lodha women. The literacy percentage of the Lodhas in this village is 71 percent. Drinking water facility is available. The villagers received 'Job Card' from the Block Development Office and are found to use this card for '100 day's work scheme per year' under the Mahatma Gandhi National Rural Employment Guarantee Act (MGNREGA). A more detailed description of this village is provided in the fifth chapter in the context of the utilization of development inputs by the Lodhas of this village.

Chakadoba (J.L No. 13)

Chakadoba is a dispersed village of Shimulpal Gram Panchjyat in Binpur II block of Paschim Medinipur district. This village is situated about 1km. from Silda---Bankura road towards south, which is inhabited by the Scheduled Tribes, like Santal, Munda and the Lodha. Most of the villagers are found to be engaged as agricultural labourers and depend on forest product collection. The agricultural lands of this village are located mainly in the upland area and are under monocrop cultivation. Nearly 70-80 percent of the villagers seasonally migrate during the time of *kharif* (November-February) and *rabi*

(April-May) crop seasons. Literacy percentage among the Lodhas is very low, especially among the females.

Amlasole (J.L No. 25)

In terms of development inputs Amlasole is one of the most neglected villages of Banspahari Gram Panchyat in Binpur II block of Paschim Medinipur. We have found that most of the inhabitants of this village are Scheduled Tribes belonging to the Lodha community. Amlasole village is situated about 25 kms. from Belpahari. The road which runs from Belpahari to Amlasole is uneven and is made by earth and stone. The village is surrounded by dense forests with hilly terrain. Most of the villagers are engaged as agricultural labourers. There is no regular public transport system in this village, so people have to walk long distance to reach the market, hospital or other public facilities. In the rainy season, the condition of the road becomes worse and there are reports of death of patients on the way to hospital. The drinking water is inadequate. There are 3 wells in surrounding area, one of them already abandoned, another is far away from the village and the remaining one, which was in the house of Somai Sabar, has stopped functioning. The village is predominantly inhabited by the tribes Lodha and Munda. The only caste group in this village is the Mahatas, who are economically in a better condition than the tribes of the village. The main sources of income of the rural poor in Amlasole or for that matter in the Banspari Gram Panchyat are the traditional weaving of ropes from *babui* grass, (*Eulaliopsis binata*) picking of *Kendu(Diospyros melanoxylon)* leaves and collection of dry wood from the forest. Most houses of the village consist of a single room with a single door without any window. The walls are either made by bricks cemented with mud or only with mud and the roofs are thatched by asbestos and/or straw. The literacy percentage of the villagers is very low, particularly among the Lodhas. The Block Development Officer reported that no work has been done in the last four years (2003-2006) under the Sampoorna Grameen Rozgar Yojana (SGRY) and Rastrya Sama Vikas Yojna (RSVY). Only four persons in this village got some relief in kind under Annapoorna and Antyoday Yojna. There is no plan for constructing roads under Pradhan Mantri Gram Swarojgar Yojna (PMGSY) scheme. The BDO also reported that the listing of poor families for the distribution of various development inputs had started in 2001, but till 2006 no BPL (Below Poverty Line) card to the beneficiary families has been distributed.

Sankhabhanga (J.L No. 157)

Sankhabhanga is a small village of Shimulpal Gram Panchayat in Binpur II block of Paschim Medinipur inhabited by only seven families. It was found that all the inhabitants belonged to the Lodha community. The village is situated 30 kms. from Belpahari. The road condition of this village is also very poor. It is made by earth and stone. When we first traveled to Sankhabhanga village by a car it was an amazing journey. It seemed as if we were going by a boat in a turbulent river or sea. Both sides of the road are covered by bushes. All the villagers depended on daily labour and forest product collection. There is no regular public transport system to this village either from Belpahari(30 kms from the village) or Odolchua (25 Kms from the village). There was no water supply system for drinking and domestic use. The health condition of the villagers is very poor. Only one family received assistance for the construction of a house under the Indira Awas Yojna of the Government. The villagers have no agricultural land although the Land and Land Reforms Department claimed to have distributed land to three families on paper. The reality is that the three beneficiary families have not seen those plots of land at the time of our fieldwork. The houses are made by mud walls and bamboo and the roof is thatched by straw, grass and leaf. The villagers did not own any domestic cattle except some poultry birds. A big rainwater harvesting tank has been constructed in the vicinity of the village under the RSVY scheme but the level of water was not adequate either for irrigation of the agricultural land or Pisciculture. The Lodhas of the village only worked as daily labour when the tank was dug. In sum, no development input has been given in a proper way in this village. The road condition, education, health facility, water supply, irrigation, sanitation and electricity are found to be in a wretched condition.

Chirakuti (J.L No. 91)

Chirakuti is a small Lodha village of Banspahari Gram Panchayat in Binpur II block of Paschim Medinipur. It was found that all inhabitants belong to the Lodha community. This village is situated 25 km from Belpahari, The road condition of this village is extremely worse. The road was made by earth and rough stone. Both side of the road are covered by bushes. The villagers mainly depend on daily labour and minor forest produce collection. There is no regular public transport system connecting the village with other places. There is no facility of drinking and domestic water supply. The health condition of the villagers was also found to be very poor. The villagers received financial assistance for constructing house under IAY, solar cell and Mid-term monetary loan from the Government as development inputs. The villagers did not possess agricultural land. The Government has distributed *patta* land on paper to three families but the fact is the beneficiaries have not seen their lands. The houses are made of mud and bamboo and the roof thatched by straw, grass and leaf. They have no domestic cattle except some poultry birds. It seemed that the development inputs have not been given in any planned manner to the beneficiaries of this village. In sum, all the basic development inputs like transport, education, health facility, water supply, irrigation, sanitation and land distribution revealed an overall dismal scenario.

Palasia (J.L No. 106)

Palasia is a village of Kharikamathani Gram Panchayat in Nayagram block of Paschim Medinipur district. Only two tribal communities, viz., Santal and Lodha inhabit this village. The village is situated about 11kms. from Kharikamathani bus road leading to Gopiballavpur towards west. It was found that only 25 Lodha families live in this village. The main source of income of the villagers is minor forest produce collection. The villagers received financial assistance for constructing their houses and they have also received agricultural land and solar cells from the Government as development inputs. There is no drinking water facility in the village. The health condition of people of this village is found to be poor. It was reported by the villagers that they have not attended any health awareness programme organised by the Gram Panchayat and Block level administration. There is no sub-health centre in the village.

Ambhisole (J.L No. 115)

Ambhisole is a village under Kharikamathani GP in Nayagram block of Paschim Medinipur district. Santals and Lodhas live in this village. This village is situated about 7 km. from Kharikamathani road which runs to Gopiballavpur towards west. Thirty two Lodha families inhabit this village. The villagers are found to be aware about the development inputs allocated by the Government. The main source of income of the villagers is minor forest produce collection. The villagers received financial assistance from the

Government to construct their houses and they also received agricultural land as well as solar cells. There are two woman self-help-groups organised by the Santals and the Lodhas. There is a non-formal school (*Sishu Siskha Kendra*) in the village established by the Government. The Lodha children are found to study in this non-formal school. The villagers are found to use water from traditional dug-wells. The inhabitants of this village were found to attend the health awareness programme organised by the Gram Panchayat and Block level administration.

Sitalpura (J.L No. 146)

Sitalpura is a village of Nayagram Gram Panchayat in Nayagram block of Paschim Medinipur district. This village is inhabited by the Santal and Lodha community. The village is situated about 5 kms. from the Nayagram GP office. Twenty nine Lodha families live in this village. The main source of income of the villagers is the collection of minor forest produce from forests lying about 5-6 kms. from the village.

Most of the villagers seasonally migrate from their homes to work as daily labourers. The panchayat has dug 10 wells in this village which serve as source of drinking water but in summer all these wells get dry. The transport system and the road conditions of the village are also very poor. The villagers received financial assistance from the Government to construct houses. They, however, have not received agricultural land from the Block Land and Land Reforms department. The village has no school and health sub-centre.

Banksole: (J.L No. 111)

Banksole is a village under Kharikamathani Gram Panchayat of Nayagram Block in Paschim Medinipur district. Mahata, Santal and Lodhas live in this village. There are thirty three Lodha families in this village.

The village is situated about 10 kms. from the Nayagram Block office. It is surrounded by dense forest. There are five dug wells constructed by the panchayat and one private tubewell from which the villagers collect water for drinking and domestic use. The main source of income of the Lodhas in Banksole is minor forest produce collection. They also work as daily labourers in the Santal and Mahata households during the agricultural season. It was found that some of the Lodha families were cultivating land as unrecorded sharecroppers of some Santal landowners.

The Lodhas of the village have also received various types of development inputs like financial assistance for house building, *patta* land and solar cells from the Government. There is a non-formal school in the village. The road condition and health care system of this village was found to be in a poor condition.

Bansiasole (J.L No. 116)

Bansiasole is a village in Kalmapukuria Gram Panchayat of Nayagram Block in Paschim Medinipur. In this village sixty five families belonging to Mahata, Santal and Lodha inhabit. There are only nineteen Lodha families in this village. The village is situated about 12 kms. from Nayagram Block office. The village is surrounded by dense forest. There are seven dug wells in the village constructed by the Gram Panchayat and the villagers use water from these wells. The main occupation of the villagers is minor forest produce collection and daily labour. There is big pond in the village which was constructed by the Government under RSVY scheme. The villagers have received various types of development inputs like financial assistance for houses building, *patta* land, Mid Term loan and cattle from the Government. The houses constructed by the district administration have only one living room with a single door without any window. The walls are made by bricks with mud and the roof thatched by asbestos and straw. The villagers had no ration card for getting food crop from the public distribution system till 2004. In 2005, they received ration cards. In this village forty persons were found to be literate. Only one person belonging to the Mahata community has a Bachelor's degree. Two Self-help-groups constituted by Lodha, Santal and Mahata were found to be functioning in this village. There is no health sub-centre; Integrated Child Development Scheme centre and the public transport system was found to be in a poor condition.

Singhdhui (J.L No. 06)

Singhdhui is a village in Patina Gram Panchayat of Nayagram Block in Paschim Medinipur which lies by the side of a metal road which runs from Gopiballavpur I to Nayagram block. We have found forty nine Lodha families in this village. The village is situated about 18 kms. from Nayagram Block Development Office. It is surrounded by dense forest. There are eight dug wells in the village and the villagers use water from these wells for drinking and domestic purposes. The main occupation of the villagers revolves around minor forest produce collection as well as agricultural and non-agricultural labour. Some Lodha families of the village were also found to be engaged in the cultivation of their own lands which they purchased from their neighbours. There are two big ponds in the village constructed by the district administration under the RSVY scheme. The villagers received various types of development inputs like financial assistance for house building, *patta* land, solar cells and Mid Term loan from the Government. The houses have only one living room with a single door without any window. The walls are made by bricks with mud and the roofs thatched by asbestos and straw. The Lodha beneficiaries of this village reported that they have sold the solar cells to some well-to-do families belonging to the caste groups of the locality. In the village, 110 persons were found to be literate. Two Self-help-groups constituted by the Lodhas were found to be functioning in the village. There is a Government primary school where the Lodha children were found to be enrolled. There are three grocery shops and four betel leaf (*paan*) shops run by the Lodhas. The villagers seasonally migrated as agricultural labourers to double crop areas of the region. There is no health sub-centre and Integrated Child Development Scheme centre in the village. The public transport system was found to be in a better condition than the other villages of Nayagram block under the study.

Demographic Contour of the Lodha Population in the Three Blocks

The total number of Lodha households in our sample is 332 and their total population is 1382.The first interesting demographic feature of the Lodha population in our study area which deserves to be mentioned is the sex -ratio that shows a clear predominance of females in this sample. The village-wise sex-ratios also show a preponderance of females over males.

At the village level, only three villages out of thirteen in our sample have more males than females. Interestingly, the highest sex -ratio is found in the Amlasole village of Binpur II in which the economic condition of the Lodhas were found to be very poor and the distribution of development inputs was far from satisfactory. (Table 2 and Figure 1).

Table 1. Block -wise Household and Population of the Lodhas

Sl. No	Block	Household	Total Population	Mean Household Size
1	Binpur II	87(26.20)	319(23.08)	3.7
2	Nayagram	182(54.82)	720(52.10)	3.9
3	Narayangarh	63(18.97)	343(24.82)	5.4
TOTAL		**332(99.99)**	**1382(100.00)**	**4.2**

Figures in parentheses represent percentages out of the column total.

Table 2. Profiles of the Surveyed Lodha Settlements

Sl.No.	Name of village	J.L. No	Male	Female	Total Population	Number of households	Mean Household size	Village wise sex ratio
1	Amlasole (Binpur II)	25	21	39	60	18	3.3	1857.14
2	Chakadoba (Binpur II)	13	25	43	68	18	3.8	1481.48
3	Chirakuthi (Binpur II)	91	20	20	40	08	5.0	1000.00
4	Dhobakacha (Binpur II)	89	20	28	48	10	4.8	1181.81
5	Rimradanga (Binpur II)	90	37	46	84	26	3.2	1243.24
6	Sankhabhanga (Binpur II)	157	10	11	20	07	2.8	1100.00
7	Ambhisole (Nayagram)	115	55	69	124	32	3.8	1254.54
8	Bansiasole (Nayagram)	116	39	36	75	19	3.9	785.71
9	Banksole (Nayagram)	111	62	66	128	33	3.9	1064.52
10	Palasia (Nayagram)	106	57	48	105	25	4.2	779.66
11	Sitalpura (Nayagram)	146	42	46	88	24	3.7	1095.24
12	Singdhui (Nayagram)	06	108	92	200	49	4.0	851.85
13	Daharpur (Narayangarh)	26	163	180	343	63	5.4	1104.29
Total	**13**		**658**	**724**	**1382**	**332**	**3.8**	**1098.63**

Sex ratio for this table is calculated by the formula: F/M X 1000.

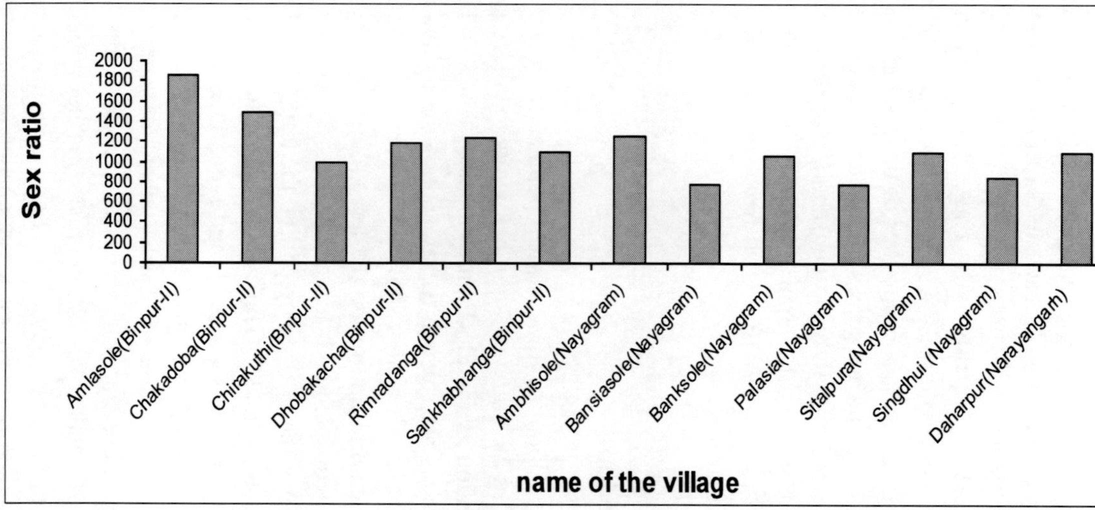

Figure 1. The Bar graph showing the village wise sex ratio.

The second interesting demographic feature of this sample is the small household size of the Lodhas. The number of Lodha settlements/villages is distributed almost equally in Binpur II, Nayagram and Narayangarh blocks. The number of households, however, is greater in Nayagram than in Binpur II and the largest Lodha settlement (49) in our sample comes from Nayagram while the smallest (07) belongs to Binpur II. These Lodha settlements have recorded an overall small household size (4.2) which is generally found among all the hunter-gatherer and landless, poor families of the rural areas. (Table 1). Among the three blocks, Narayangarh shows the highest mean household size (5.4) which is higher than the overall mean household size of our sample. At the village level, only one village of Binpur II shows a household size 5, but all the other villages of Nayagram and Binpur II have household sizes ranging between 2.8- 4.8. (Table 2).

The Age-Sex Composition

The age -sex composition of the sample population revealed higher number of younger persons including children belonging to 0-4, 5-9 and 10-14 age groups. The population pyramid (Figure 1) also shows a broad base extending up to 15-19 years, after which the breadth of the pyramid began to shrink although, the number of females showed a sudden increase at the age group 25-29 which seemed unusual. In the old age groups, i.e., above 65, the absence of women is conspicuous. It seems that although there is a preponderance of females in the Lodha population, the longevity of the Lodha women is much lesser than the males. This pattern is also found in case of all the three blocks when considered separately, and scenario is worst in Binpur II. In general, the female population in the higher age groups, particularly beyond the reproductive age, i.e., after 49 years, showed a greater number than the males. We, however, have not found any female above the age group 65-69 but there were 10 males above 69 years in the population. The interesting aspect about the demography of the Lodhas in this sample (which we have already noted) is the preponderance of females in almost all the age groups (the sex ratio being 1100). This fact is most revealing in all the younger age groups from 0-4 up to 35-39.Only in the age groups 40-44 and 45-49, we have found a predominance of males over females (Tables 3 and 4 and Figure 2). If we consider the three blocks separately, then we find that the aggregate sex-ratios in Binpur II and Narayangarh are in favour of the females, whereas, in the Nayagram block the overall sex-ratio is in favour of the males except in the age group 65-69 in which the females predominate.(Tables 6, 8,10 and Figures 3,4,5).

Table 3. Age-sex Composition of the Lodhas in Three Administrative Blocks of Paschim Medinipur District

Age Group	Male	Female	Total
0-4	[12.77] 84 (6.08)	[12.98] 94 (6.80)	178 (12.88)
5-9	[11.85] 78 (5.64)	[14.23] 103 (7.45)	181 (13.10)
10-14	[10.33] 68 (4.92)	[8.84] 64 (4.63)	132 (9.55)
15-19	[8.21] 54 (3.91)	[7.87] 57 (4.12)	111 (8.03)
20-24	[7.45] 49 (3.55)	[7.32] 53 (3.83)	102 (7.38)
5-29	[7.60] 50 (3.62)	[11.33] 82 (5.93)	132 (9.55)
30-34	[7.90] 52 (3.76)	[8.98] 65 (4.70)	117 (8.47)
35-39	[8.97] 59 (4.27)	[8.15] 59 (4.27)	118 (8.54)
40-44	[8.21] 54 (3.91)	[5.52] 40 (2.89)	94 (6.80)
45-49	[6.38] 42 (3.04)	[3.59] 26 (1.88)	68 (4.92)
50-54	[3.04] 20 (1.45)	[4.42] 32 (2.32)	52 (3.76)
55-59	[2.28] 15 (1.09)	[3.18] 23 (1.66)	38 (2.75)
60-64	[2.74] 18 (1.30)	[2.62] 19 (1.37)	37 (2.68)
65-69	[0.76] 05 (0.36)	[0.97] 07 (0.51)	12 (0.87)
70-74	[0.91] 06 (0.43)	00	6 (0.43)
75-79	[0.30] 02 (0.14)	00	2 (0.14)
80+	[0.30] 02 (0.14)	00	2 (0.14)
Total	**[100.00] 658 (47.61)**	**[100.00] 724 (52.39)**	**1382 (100.00)**

[ ] Represents percentage out of column total. ( ) Represents percentage out of grand total.

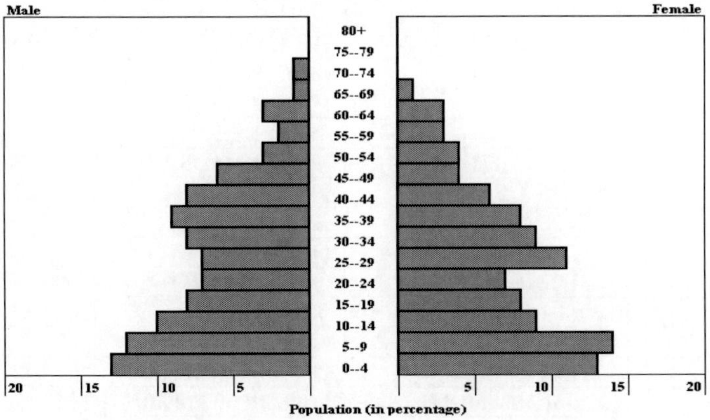

Figure 2. The Population pyramid of the study population.

Table 4. Age Group wise Sex Ratio of the Lodhas in the Total Population

Age group	Male	Female	Sex ratio
0-4	84	94	1119
5-9	78	103	1321
10-14	68	64	941
15-19	54	57	1056
20-24	49	53	1082
25-29	50	82	1640
30-34	52	65	1250
35-39	59	59	1000
40-44	54	40	741
45-49	42	26	619
50-54	20	32	1600
55-59	15	23	1533
60-64	18	19	1056
65-69	05	07	1400
70-74	06	00	0
75-79	02	00	0
80+	02	00	0
Total	**658**	**724**	**1100**

Table 5. Age-sex Composition of six Lodha Villages in Nayagram Block

Age group	Male	Female	Total
0-4	[16.26] 60 (8.33)	[16.14] 57 (7.91)	117 (16.25)
5-9	[12.26] 45 (6.25)	[14.16] 50 (6.94)	95 (13.19)
10-14	[10.08] 37 (5.14)	[8.21] 29 (4.02)	66 (9.17)
15-19	[7.63] 28 (3.84)	[10.19] 36 (5.00)	64 (8.89)
20-24	[5.72] 21 (2.92)	[7.93] 28 (3.89)	49 (6.80)
25-29	[9.26] 34 (4.725)	[10.48] 37 (5.13)	71 (9.86)
30-34	[8.17] 30 (4.16)	[8.49] 30 (4.16)	60 (8.33)
35-39	[7.08] 26 (3.61)	[7.65] 27 (3.75)	53 (7.33)
40-44	[7.62] 28 (3.88)	[4.24] 15 (2.08)	43 (5.97)
45-49	[6.81] 25 (3.47)	[2.83] 10 (1.38)	35 (4.86)
50-54	[1.63] 06 (0.83)	[3.39] 12 (1.66)	18 (2.50)
55-59	[2.17] 08 (1.11)	[2.54] 09 (1.25)	17 (2.36)
60-64	[4.08] 15 (2.08)	[1.69] 06 (0.83)	21 (2.91)
65-69	[0.54] 02 (0.27)	[1.98] 07 (0.97)	09 (1.25)
70-74	[0.27] 01 (0.13)	00	01 (0.13)
75-79	00	00	00
80+	[0.27] 01 (0.13)	00	01 (0.13)
Total	**[100.00] 367 (50.97)**	**[100.00] 353 (49.03)**	**720 (100.00)**

[ ] Represents percentage out of column total. ( ) Represents percentage out of grand total.

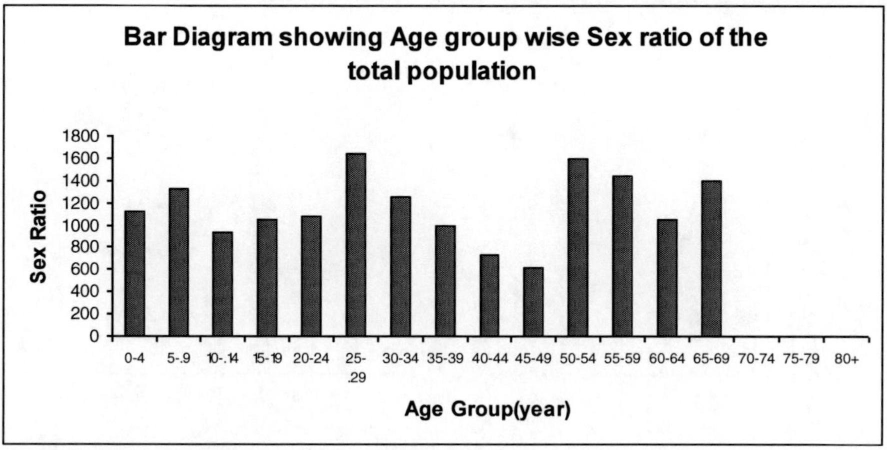

Figure 3. The Bar Diagram showing Age group wise Sex ratio of the total population.

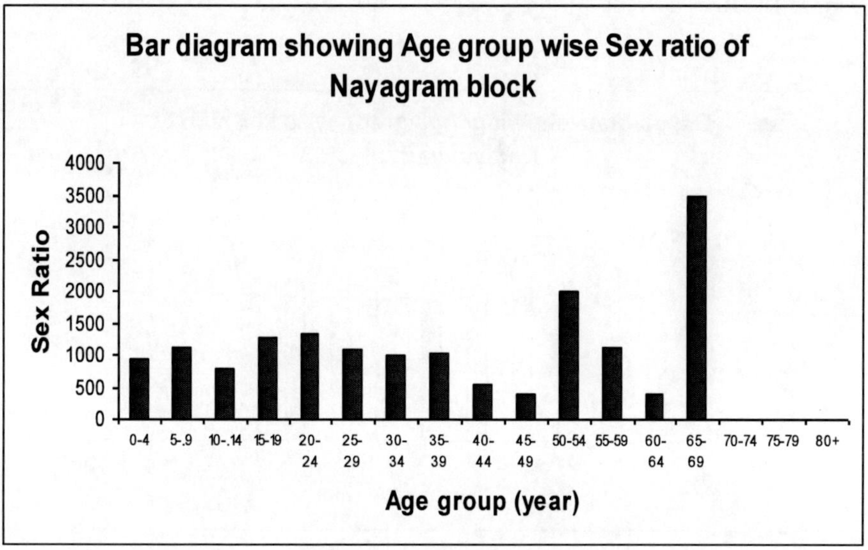

Figure 4. The Bar diagram showing age group wise sex ratio of Nayagram block.

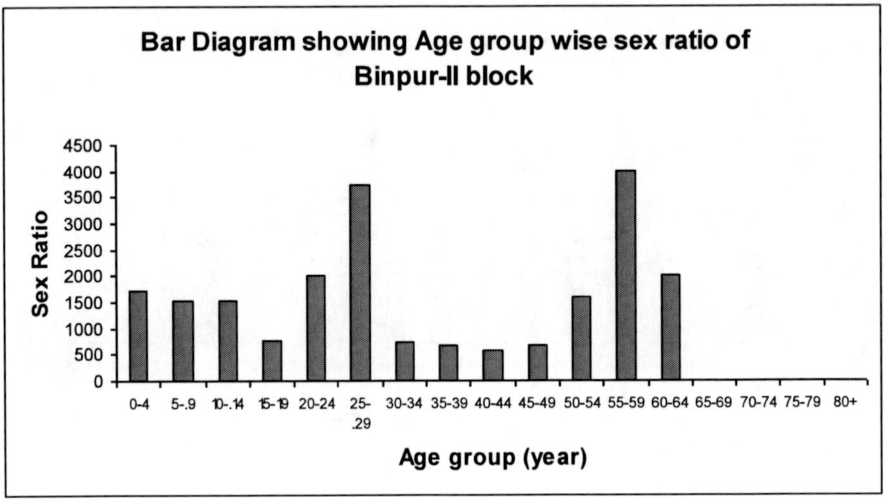

Figure 5. The Bar Diagram showing age group wise sex ratio of Binpur-II block.

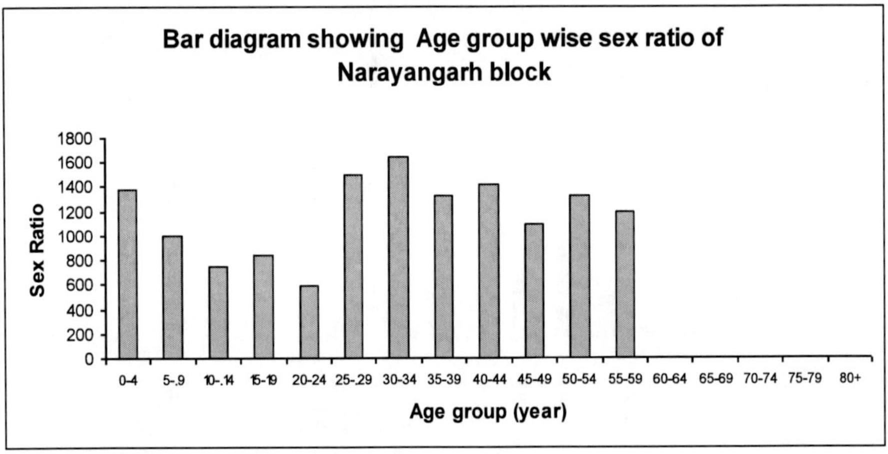

Figure 6. The Bar diagram showing age group wise Sex ratio of Nayagram block.

Table 6. Age group wise sex -ratio of the Lodhas of Nayagram Block

Age group	Male	Female	Sex-ratio
0-4	60	57	950
5-9	45	50	1111
10-14	37	29	784
15-19	28	36	1286
20-24	21	28	1333
25-29	34	37	1088
30-34	30	30	1000
35-39	26	27	1038
40-44	28	15	536
45-49	25	10	400
50-54	06	12	2000
55-59	08	09	1125
60-64	15	06	400
65-69	02	07	3500
70-74	01	00	0
75-79	00	00	0
80+	01	00	0
Total	**367**	**353**	**962**

Table 7. Age-sex Composition of six Lodha Villages in Binpur II Block

Age group	Male	Female	Total
0-4	(3.45) 11 [7.97]	(5.96) 19 [1050]	30(9.40)
5-9	(5.96) 19 [13.77]	(9.09) 29 [16.02]	48(15.05)
10-14	(4.70) 15 [10.87]	(7.21) 23 [12.71]	38(11.91)
15-19	(4.08) 13 [9.42]	(3.13) 10 [5.52]	23(7.21)
20-24	(1.88) 06 [4.35]	(3.76) 12 [6.63]	18(5.64)
5-29	(2.51) 08 [5.80]	(9.40) 30 [16.57]	38(11.91)
30-34	(5.02) 16 [11.59]	(3.76) 12 [6.63]	28(8.78)
35-39	(5.64) 18 [13.04]	(3.76) 12 [6.63]	30(9.40)
40-44	(4.39) 14 [10.14]	(2.51) 08 [4.42]	22(6.90)
45-49	(1.88) 06 [4.35]	(1.25) 04 [2.21]	10(3.13)
50-54	(1.57) 05 [3.62]	(2.51) 08 [4.42]	13(4.08)
55-59	(0.63) 02 [1.45]	(2.51) 08 [4.42]	10(3.13)
60-64	(0.94) 03 [2.17]	(1.88) 06 [3.31]	09(2.82)
65-69			0.00
70-74	(0.31) 01 [0.72]		01(0.31)
75-79			0.00
80+	(0.31) 01 [0.72]		01(0.31)
Total	**(43.26)138[100.00]**	**(56.74) 181 [100.00]**	**319(100.00)**

[ ] Represents percentage out of column total. ( ) Represents percentage out of grand total.

Table 8. Age group wise sex -ratio of the Lodhas of Binpur II Block

Age group	Male	Female	Sex ratio
0-4	11	19	1727
5-9	19	29	1526
10-14	15	23	1533
15-19	13	10	769
20-24	06	12	2000
5-29	08	30	3750
30-34	16	12	750
35-39	18	12	667
40-44	14	08	571
45-49	06	04	667
50-54	05	08	1600
55-59	02	08	4000
60-64	03	06	2000
65-69			0
70-74	01		0
75-79			0
80+	01		0
Total	**138**	**181**	**1312**

Table 9. Age-sex Composition of the Lodhas in Narayangarh Block

Age group	Male	Female	Total
0-4	(3.79) 13 [7.98]	(5.25) 18 [10.00]	31[9.04]
5-9	(4.08) 14 [8.59]	(4.08) 14 [7.78]	28[8.16]
10-14	(4.66) 16 [9.82]	(3.50) 12 [6.67]	28[8.16]
15-19	(3.79) 13 [7.98]	(3.21) 11 [6.11]	24[7.00]
20-24	(6.41) 22 [13.50]	(3.79) 13 [7.22]	35[10.20]
5-29	(2.92) 10 [6.13]	(4.37) 15 [8.33]	25[7.29]
30-34	(4.08) 14 [8.59]	(6.71) 23 [12.78]	37[10.79]
35-39	(4.37) 15 [9.20]	(5.83) 20 [11.11]	35[10.20]
40-44	(3.50) 12 [7.36]	(4.96) 17 [9.44]	29[8.45]
45-49	(3.21) 11 [6.75]	(3.50) 12 [6.67]	23[6.71]
50-54	(2.62) 09 [5.52]	(3.50) 12 [6.67]	21[6.12]
55-59	(1.46) 05 [3.07]	(1.75) 06 [3.33]	11[3.21]
60-64	(0.00) 00 [0.00]	(2.04) 07 [3.89]	07[2.04]
65-69	(0.87) 03 [1.84]	00	03[0.87]
70-74	(1.17) 04 [2.45]	00	04[1.17]
75-79	(0.58) 02 [1.23]	00	02[0.58]
80+	(0.00) 00 [0.00]	00	00[0.00]
Total	**(47.52) 163 [100.00]**	**(52.48) 180 [100.00]**	**343[100.00]**

[] Represents percentage out of column total. () Represents percentage out of grand total.

Table 10. Age group wise sex ratio of the Lodhas of Narayangarh Block

Age group	Male	Female	Sex ratio
0-4	13	18	1385
5-9	14	14	1000
10-14	16	12	750
15-19	13	11	846
20-24	22	13	591
25-29	10	15	1500
30-34	14	23	1643
35-39	15	20	1333
40-44	12	17	1417
45-49	11	12	1091
50-54	09	12	1333
55-59	05	06	1200
60-64	00	07	0
65-69	03	00	0
70-74	04	00	0
75-79	02	00	0
80+	00	00	0
Total	**163**	**180**	**1104**

Marital Status

Marriage is a universal phenomenon among the Lodhas of our study area. No person remained unmarried after the age of 39, although variation in the beginning of marriage is noticed between the sexes. The females are found to marry at an early age than the males. But the interesting fact is we have found unmarried females at higher age groups. On the other hand, the number of widows is greater than the number of widowers in the study population. (Table 11)

Literacy Status

Table 12 and Figure 6 represent the age group wise literacy condition among the Lodha population in the study area. The overall literacy condition is not very satisfactory (43.35 %) and the condition of the females in this regard is worse than the males.

Table 11. Age group wise Marital Status among the Lodhas in the three Administrative blocks

Age group	Male			Female		
	Unmarried	Married	Widower	Unmarried	Married	Widow
0-4	83(27.95)			105(38.60)		
5-9	78(26.26)			88(32.35)		
10-14	68(22.90)			54(19.85)	07(1.86)	
15-19	45(14.81)	15(4.08)		13(4.78)	42(11.14)	
20-24	18(6.06)	30(8.15)		06(2.21)	47(12.47)	01(1.54)
25-29	06(2.02)	46(12.50)		03(1.10)	78(20.69)	01(1.54)
30-34		57(15.49)		02(0.74)	57(15.12)	05(7.69)
35-39		57(15.49)		01(0.37)	53(14.06)	06(9.23)
40-44		54(14.67)			34(9.02)	05(7.69)
45-49		42(11.41)			26(6.90)	06(9.23)
50-54		20(5.43)	01(50.00)		15(3.98)	11(16.92)
55-59		15(4.08)	01(50.00)		10(2.65)	13(20.00)
60-64		19(5.16)			08(2.12)	12(18.46)
65-69		05(1.36)				05(7.69)
70-74		05(1.36)				
75-79		02(0.54)				
80+		01(0.27)				
Total	**298(100.00) [21.56]**	**368(100.00) [26.63]**	**02(100.00) [0.14]**	**272(100.00) [19.68]**	**377(100.00) [27.28]**	**65(100.00) [4.70]**

[ ] Represents percentage out of column total. ( ) Represents percentage out of grand total.

Table 12. Age group wise Literacy Status of the Lodha Population in three Administrative Blocks

Age group	Male			Female		
	Illiterate	Literate	Total	Illiterate	Literate	Total
0-4	[25.64]80(5.79)		80	[20.17]95(6.87)		95
5-9	[10.58]33(2.39)	[11.82]41(2.97)	74	[11.46]54(3.91)	[15.48]39(2.82)	93
10-14	[4.81]15(1.08)	[15.56]54(3.91)	69	[6.37]30(2.17)	[12.70]32(2.32)	62
15-19	[5.13]16(1.15)	[9.80]34(2.46)	50	[6.37]30(2.17)	[10.71]27(1.95)	57
20-24	[2.88]09(0.65)	[10.37]36(2.60)	45	[7.01]33(2.39)	[9.13]23(1.66)	56
25-29	[4.81]15(1.08)	[11.82]41(2.97)	56	[12.31]58(4.20)	[11.51]29(2.09)	87
30-34	[9.94]31(2.24)	[8.93]31(2.24)	62	[7.01]33(2.39)	[13.10]33(2.39)	66
35-39	[7.37]23(1.66)	[9.80]34(2.46)	57	[7.43]35(2.53)	[9.92]25(1.81)	60
40-44	[8.65]27(1.95)	[8.65]30(2.17)	57	[4.88]23(1.66)	[5.95]15(1.08)	38
45-49	[6.41]20(1.44)	[6.05]20(1.44)	40	[3.40]16(1.16)	[5.16]14(1.01)	30
50-54	[4.17]13(0.94)	[2.02]07(0.51)	20	[4.46]21(1.52)	[5.16]13(0.94)	34
55-59	[4.49]14(1.01)	[2.59]09(0.65)	23	[3.82]18(1.30)	[1.19]03(0.22)	21
60-64	[0.96]03(0.21)	[1.73]06(0.43)	09	[4.25]20(1.45)		20
65-69	[1.60]05(0.36)	[0.86]03(0.22)	08	[1.06]05(0.36)		05
70-74	[1.92]06(0.43)	00	06			
75-79	[0.64]02(0.14)	00	02			
80+		00				
Total	**[100.00]312(22.58)**	**[100.00]346(25.04)**	**658**	**[100.00]471(34.08)**	**[100.00]253(18.31)**	**724**

[ ] Represents percentage out of column total. ( ) Represents percentage out of grand total.

The table shows that 22.58 percent males are illiterate and 25.11 percent are literate out of the total population whereas the same figures for the females are 34.08 and 18.23 percent respectively out of the total population. The percentage of illiterate persons in the early school going age groups (5-14) is higher among the females. The highest number of literate individuals is found among the males in the age group 10-14 while among the females it is in the age group 5-9. An upward trend of the number of literate persons in both sexes is observed from the higher to lower age groups indicating the fact that the younger Lodhas are gradually showing interest to become literate.

In this table a detailed break-up of the literacy status of the Lodha population has been done. The interesting feature which is revealed from this table is the trend of literacy level in the different age categories. It is found that the percentage of Lodha male and female population in the primary level rises to 9.91 and 8.24 respectively when compared with the category 'Can sign'. The percentage of people declines consistently in the subsequent higher levels of educational categories. The fall in the percentage becomes remarkable at the class IX and above for the females.

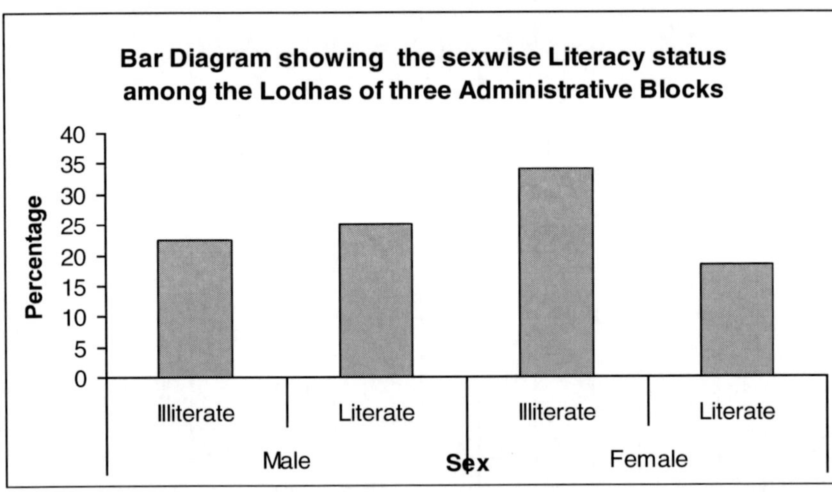

Figure 7. Bar Diagram showing the sex wise Literacy status among the Lodhas of three Administrative Blocks.

The break-up of the detailed literacy condition of the population into bigger age categories also revealed that the younger Lodhas have achieved more primary education than the older persons. This is true for the primary and junior high school levels. The contribution of younger age groups is also remarkably higher beyond the post junior high levels (eight standard) of school education, although there is a considerable difference between the males and females at this level. The frequency polygon s of the three age also shows a more-or-less consistent trend of rise and fall among the males and females with slight variations (Figures 7, 8 and 9).

The household size of the Lodhas in the surveyed population reveals a predominance of small households ranging between 4-6 persons; the mean household size being 4.2. The small household size of the population may be viewed in the context of the subsistence pattern of the Lodhas. We have observed that the majority of the individuals (47.03%) are engaged in forest produce collection to earn their livelihood. Only two persons were engaged in service. A substantial number of individuals (43.05%) were found to be engaged in agricultural as well as non agricultural labour. About 130 households have been found to be engaged in the cultivation of their own land. This however, constitutes only 9.07 percent of total number of households of the study area. (Tables 15 and 16).

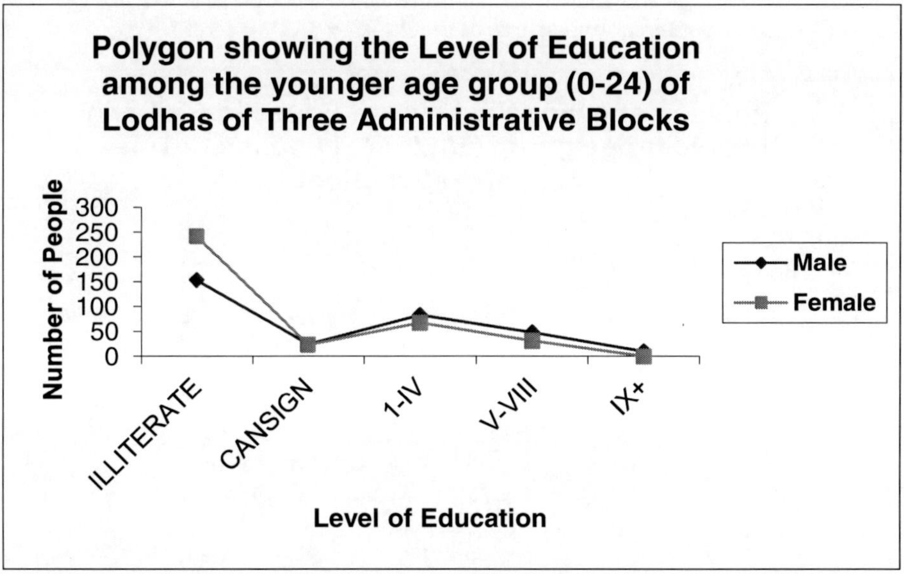

Figure 8. Polygon showing the Level of Education among the younger age group (0-24) of Lodhas of three Administrative Blocks.

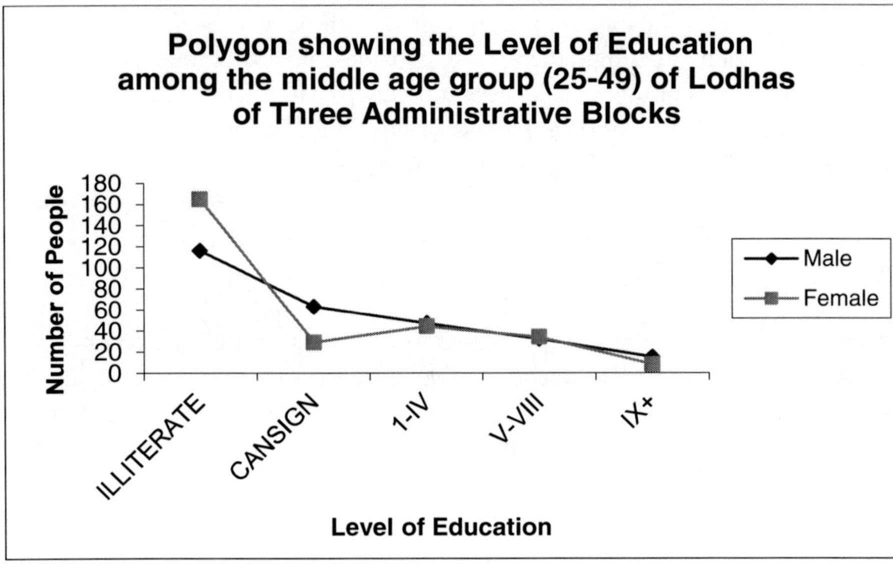

Figure 9. The Polygon showing the Level of Education among the middle age group (25-49) of Lodhas of three Administrative Blocks.

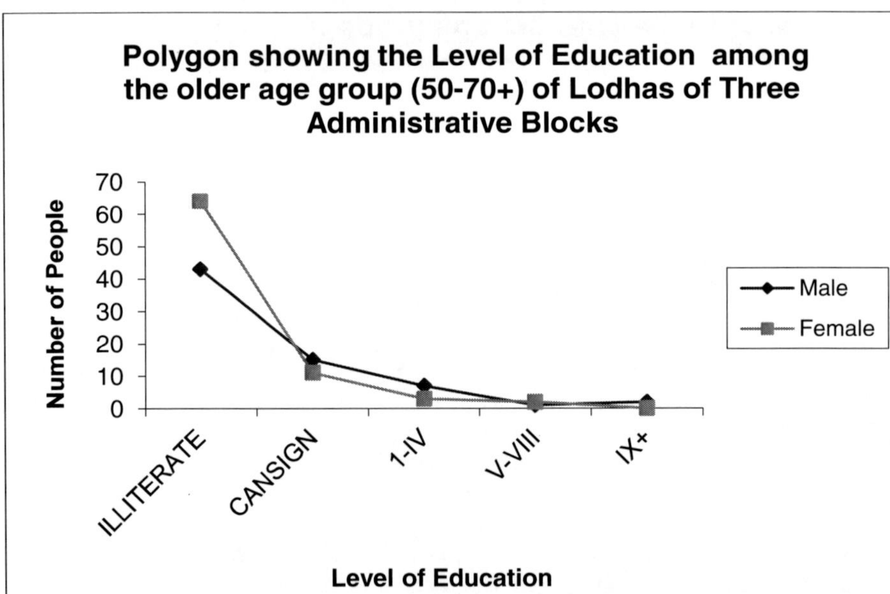

Figure 10. Polygon showing the Level of Education among the older age group (50-70+) of Lodhas of the three Administrative Blocks.

Table 13. Level of Education among the Lodhas of three Administrative Blocks according to the age and sex in the study area

Age group	ILLITERATE		CAN SIGN		1-IV		V-VIII		IX+	
	Male	Female	Male	Female	Male	Female	Male	Female	Male	Female
0-4	80	95	00	00	00	00	00	00	00	00
5-9	33	54	07	07	34	32	00	00	00	00
10-14	15	30	02	05	29	14	20	13	03	00
15-19	16	30	07	05	07	10	16	12	04	00
20-24	09	33	08	06	13	11	12	06	03	00
25-29	15	58	17	07	13	13	06	07	05	02
30-34	31	33	16	09	08	13	04	09	03	02
35-39	23	35	07	03	10	09	11	09	06	04
40-44	27	23	12	05	09	06	08	04	01	00
45-49	20	16	11	05	07	03	03	05	00	00
50-54	13	21	03	09	04	02	00	02	00	00
55-59	14	18	05	02	02	01	00	00	02	00
60-64	03	20	05	00	01	00	00	00	00	00
65-69	05	05	02	00	00	00	01	00	00	00
70+	08	00	00	00	00	00	00	00	00	00
Total	**312 (22.58)**	**471 (34.08)**	**102 (7.38)**	**63 (4.56)**	**137 (9.91)**	**114 (8.24)**	**81 (5.86)**	**67 (4.85)**	**27 (1.95)**	**08 (0.58)**

Figures in parentheses represent percentages.

Table 14. Level of Education among the Lodhas of three Administrative Blocks According to three major age Categories

Age group	Category	ILLITERATE	CAN SIGN	I-IV	V-VIII	IX+
0-24	Male	153	24	83	48	10
	Female	242	23	67	31	00
25-49	Male	116	63	47	32	15
	Female	165	29	44	34	08
50-70+	Male	43	15	07	01	02
	Female	64	11	03	02	00
Total		**783(56.66)**	**165(11.94)**	**252(18.23)**	**146(10.56)**	**35(2.53)**

Figures in parentheses represent percentage out of the total population (1382) of the study area.

Household Size and Subsistence Pattern

Table 15. Household size of the Lodhas in the study area

Category	Total number of household	
1-3	141(42.47)	**Mean Household Size**
4-6	164(49.40)	4.2
7+	27(8.13)	
Total	332	

Figures in parentheses represent percentages.

Table 16. Subsistence Pattern of the Lodhas in the study area

Cultivation	Agricultural labor	Non-agricultural labor	Forest produce collection	Service	Total
130(9.07)	352(24.56)	265(18.49)	674(47.03)	12(0.84)	1433

Figures in parentheses represent percentages.

It is observed that the Lodhas in our study area are mostly engaged in forest produce collection and they were also found to be working as labourers in the agricultural and non-agricultural sector s. A small number of Lodha families were found to cultivate their own land and a much smaller number of them were engaged in the service sector.

Chapter IV

THE DEVELOPMENT INPUTS AND THE ROLE OF THE STATE

THE GOVERNMENTAL PERSPECTIVE OF DEVELOPEMENT AMONG THE LODHAS

In the post-Independence period the main aim of the Government was to put off the stigma of criminal tribe designation of the Lodhas. At the same time the Government also sought to uplift the socio-economic condition of this tribe who mainly depended on forest produce and daily labour. Another important component of the governmental perspective centering round the development of the Lodhas was to settle this tribe as an agriculturist population. The approach of the non-governmental organizations was not different from the government in this regard. The applied anthropological efforts made by Probodh Kumar Bhowmick also centered round the resettlement of Lodhas as settled agriculturists. For this reason, every effort to improve the condition of the Lodhas consisted of giving them land, permanent houses, domestic animals and poultry birds. There was virtually no effort on the part of the Government and the NGOs to improve the economy of the Lodhas within the fold of the forests which the members of this tribe knew best. The traditional and intimate knowledge of the Lodhas about the forest and the animals and plants on which the community sustained its livelihood were rarely studied and used by the governmental and non-governmental development agencies. Even the anthropologists, who have studied the Lodhas, did not study the relationship of the Lodhas with the forests in detail. One striking fact in this regard is the virtual neglect of the Lodhas by the

Forest Department of the Government. For example, in the joint forest management movement the participation of the Lodhas is still very much negligible. Most of the benefits gained through the activities of the Forest Protection Committee s are enjoyed by the members of the economically and socially dominant castes and tribes. This truncated approach towards the development of the Lodhas operated in such a manner that the socio-economic condition of the tribe did not improve appreciably in the long post-Independence period. As a result of the failure of the Government to improve the condition of the Lodhas and other tribes under similar conditions, the Government of India coined a new designation for such tribes in the year 1971 for their development, which was 'Primitive Tribal Group' or PTG. The Lodhas of West Bengal were put under this new category. The overall approach towards the development of the Lodhas however, did not change much after the introduction of this new designation, except for the fact that more funds for the development of the Lodhas were allocated. In a later period, another new idea for the development of the 'backward districts' came into existence. This scheme was launched by the Planning Commission of India and it is known as the Rastriya Sama Vikas Yojna (RSVY).

The scheme aimed at focused development programmes for backward areas which, it was thought, would help reduce imbalances and speed up development.Under the RSVY scheme, the Central Government aimed to cover one hundred backward districts in India. Already fifty backward districts have been covered during 2003-2004 and a sum of Rs.15000 crore per year was provided to each of the district for a period of three years, that is a total of Rs. 45.00 crore per district have been released to the State Government s on hundred percent grant basis in installment. The Paschim Medinipur District was identified as a backward district and a grant from the RSVY scheme was released during the annual plan period 2003-2004(Planning Commission 2004). The plan document revealed that the main objective of the RSVY scheme would be to address the problems of low agricultural productivity, unemployment in the rural areas, and to fill in the critical gaps in the physical and social infrastructure s of the 'Backward region'. There is a scope in the scheme to make plans to improve the socio-economic conditions of the 'poorer pockets' and/or specific disadvantaged groups and communities. Accordingly, Paschim Medinipur district was identified as one of the 'Backward district' of West Bengal under the RSVY scheme and the district administration decided to target the Lodhas of the district for the implementation of the scheme.

The RSVY plan document has mentioned the special focus areas of development which should be undertaken in the district plan. These special focus areas are: (i) land and water management including check dams, revitalisation of traditional water structure s, small lift irrigation projects, mini diversion weirs, etc., (ii) health infrastructure, particularly strengthening of women and child development centers and provision of facilities for institutional deliveries, (iii) educational infrastructure, which would aim towards vocational training and skill development, (iv) increase in income from agriculture and allied activities through intensification of agricultural and horticultural practices, and (v) rearing of domestic animals, poultry birds and pisciculture, etc. through back-up of veterinary facilities and marketing infrastructure.

Under this general background of the governmental perspective on the development of the Lodhas, we began our research in Binpur II and Nayagram blocks of Paschim Medinipur district during 2005 firstly by identifying the different types of development inputs given to the Lodhas by the district administration under the RSVY scheme. Later in course of our fieldwork, it came to our notice that apart from the RSVY scheme various other schemes were also being implemented for the socio-economic development of the tribe. At a much later period of our research we selected the third Lodha settlement in the Narayangarh block.

During our fieldwork at Binpur II and Nayagram, we have found that although the plan of the Government was to bring the Lodhas into the fold of agriculture and settle them like a group of farmers, the distribution of land by the Land and Land Reforms Department to the landless Lodha families largely remained an unfinished task.

Our findings in the field showed that the distribution of land to the Lodhas was rarely taken up seriously as one of the major and fundamental tasks towards their socio-economic development. It was found that the Lodhas in the Binpur II and Nayagram blocks depended on the collection of forest produce in a substantial manner.

In the month of November 2005, we conducted a social anthropological fieldwork in connection with a research project on 'Socio-economic Impact Assessment of Development Programmes. Among the Lodha/Sabar of Binpur II and Nayagram Block of Paschim (West) Medinipur District ' under the *Rastriya Sama Vikas Yojana* scheme of Paschim Medinipur district sponsored by the Planning Commission of India. The project was sanctioned by the then District Magistrate of Paschim (West) Medinipur. Data on the development inputs given to Lodhas were collected for this project and an impact assessment report was also submitted to the District Magistrate in 2006.The following sections are based on the data collected for the project and also on further fieldwork done by the first author for his doctoral dissertation in Anthropology submitted to Vidyasagar University in 2012. We would now present our empirical findings as regards the distribution and utilization of various developmental inputs among the Lodha families in the three selected administrative blocks of Paschim Medinipur district. Before we present our empirical findings the methodology adopted for the research is described in the next section.

Methodology of the Research

The primary data for the research have been collected through intensive anthropological fieldwork conducted for about two consecutive years. These data included qualitative and quantitative information collected through household census, structured and unstructured questionnaire schedules and also with the help of genealogy, case study, participatory observation, focus group discussion, and panel interviews.

The fieldwork for this research was carried out from a micro-level perspective by using traditional anthropological methods like participant observation and collection of case studies. Data on the demographic, economic, political and socio-cultural dimensions of the selected Lodha settlements were also collected in the study areas.

Besides, archival data from the Government offices have also been collected which included basic background information on the delivery and utilization of various developmental programmes (including programmes under *Rastriya Sama Vikas Yojana* scheme sponsored by the Planning Commission of the Central Government). The Lodha village settlement clusters were selected on the basis of our previous field experiences in the area. Attempts were made to cover all the Lodha village/settlement clusters in which some kind of development inputs have reached.

The empirical data for the research have been collected from three hundred thirty two (332) Lodha households (the total population is 1382) in the three blocks, viz., Binpur II, Nayagram and Narayangargh. The fieldwork was conducted during 2005-06 and 2008-2012. The quantitative data collected for this research have been analyzed by using simple descriptive methods (e.g., frequency distribution tables, bar graphs, histogram s and polygons) with the help of Microsoft Excel programme. The qualitative data have been analyzed through descriptions supported by some representative case studies. A schematic diagram of the research design is given below.

The Structure of Research Design

Objectives	**LEVEL I**	**LEVEL II**	**LEVEL III**
	Listing of development inputs and collection of socio-demographic and economic data.(Mainly quantitative data)	Collection of data on the utilization of development inputs and views of the Lodhas towards them (Mainly qualitative data)	Assessment of the Impact of development inputs through comparison(a combination of qualitative and quantitative data)
Methods and Techniques Employed	1. Household Census. 2. Genealogy 3. Interview with structured and unstructured schedules 4. Observation 5. Collection of data from district administrative departments.	1. Structured and unstructured schedules 2. Focus group discussions. 3. Panel interviews. 4. Observation.	1. Group Discussions. 2. Reading of Literature. 3. Panel interviews.

DEVELOPMENT INPUTS AND UTILIZATION

In the following table we have identified all the development inputs given to the Lodhas in terms of their source and percentage of the beneficiary families. It is notable that only 41 percent of the Lodha families in the study area received some kind of development inputs from the Government which means that despite the launching of various kinds of schemes, more than half of the Lodha families were not being covered by any kind of development programme. The next important finding is, of all the thirteen types of development inputs the distribution of land to the landless families occupied only nine percent of the development inputs given to the Lodha families in the study area. The third notable finding is the lack of Government initiative towards skill development through training among the beneficiary families; only six persons were given training by the panchayats. Almost no development input was found to be given to the Lodhas of the study area as regards marketing and value addition of the minor forest produce. Some beneficiaries, however, were given loan for *babui* grass cultivation which grows on degraded forest lands. It is revealed from the scenario of development inputs that Government's attention was mostly directed to provide house, job card distribution and installation of solar cells to the beneficiary families. More than thirty percent of the beneficiaries (nearly thirteen percent of the total population) were given financial assistance to build their houses and around nineteen percent of the beneficiaries received solar cells. (Table 17)

Table 17. Types of Development inputs and the Percentage of Lodha Beneficiaries in the study area

Sl. No	Name of Development inputs	Source	Number of Beneficiary
1	Patta Land given by Government	Block Development Office	(3.26)45[7.95]
2	Land given by NGO	*Institute of Social Research and Applied Anthropology* (ISRAA)	(0.72)10[1.77]
3	House	Block Development Office	(12.66)175[30.92]
4	Job card	Panchayat(MGNREGA)	(8.32)115[20.32]
5	Pond	Panchayat(MGNREGA)	(0.29)04[0.71]
6	Money for domestic animal	Self-Help-Group	(1.01)14[2.47]
7	Training for skill development	Panchayat	(0.43)06[1.06]
8	Husking Machine & Spray Machine	Block Development Office	(0.79)11[1.94]

Sl. No	Name of Development inputs	Source	Number of Beneficiary
9	Loan (MT & Babui Cultivation)	Block Development Office	(2.46)34[6.01]
10	Old age Pension	Block Development Office	(1.16)16[2.83]
11	Solar	Block Development Office	(7.60)105[18.55]
12	Cattle	Block Development Office	(1.95)27[4.77]
13	Blanket	Block Development Office	(0.29)04[0.71]
Total Population 1382			**(40.95)566**

[ ] Figures in parentheses represent percentages out of the total household's beneficiaries.
( ) Figures in parentheses represent percentages out of the total population.

The Distribution of Development Inputs and Their Utilization

The following tables (18 A and B) shows the pattern of distribution of various types of developmental inputs given to the beneficiaries in the surveyed population. The developmental inputs under the *Rastriya Sama Vikas Yojana* (RSVY) and *Indira Awas Yojana* (IAY) schemes included (i) non-refundable cash loan for building house, (ii) solar cells for domestic use, (iii) cattle (cow, goat and bullock) and poultry birds, (iv) husking and spray machine for agricultural purpose, (v) job card, and (vi) money for domestic animal etc. We have also included the distribution of plots of agricultural land under developmental input. Our findings revealed that at the time of our survey 402(29.09%) beneficiary families out of 1382 have received various types of developmental inputs in different combination. The nature of distribution of developmental inputs by the Government shows that emphasis was given to cash loan for house building and high technology solar cells. Through our observation and interviews with the beneficiaries we have found that most of the houses were built in a hurried manner and seemed to be weak in structure. The beneficiaries also expressed their dissatisfaction with the newly built houses. We have also found that the majority of the beneficiaries who received solar cells either sold them against cash to well-to-do neighbours belonging to other communities or could not use them properly (Panda and Guha, 2009:69-75). Little attention was paid to strengthen the household level economic base of the Lodhas through a proper distribution of agricultural land and other related inputs like ploughs, irrigation water, manure and pesticide. There was no effort on the part of the agriculture department to train the beneficiaries in cultivation. As regards skill development through training, we have found that only six persons were given training and that too was done in the Narayangarh block. Training was given to middle-aged men in mushroom cultivation and micro-credit. Mushroom seeds were given to persons but no arrangement was made in their houses so that they could grow the seeds under proper condition. The persons trained in mushroom cultivation finally consumed the seeds and the training could not be utilised in future. The same persons however could use the training imparted to them on micro-credit since there were already ten women self-help-groups in the village. The distribution of cattle and poultry birds among the Lodhas of our survey population also revealed that the beneficiaries could not manage their cattle and birds owing to lack of basic knowledge in rearing those animals. As a result, it was found that many cattle, particularly goats have died within a short period of time after those were given to the beneficiaries. The beneficiaries of old age pension scheme complained to us about the delayed payment of pension by the concerned department of the Government. The overall scenario of the utilization of the various development inputs shows that the majority of the beneficiaries have utilised the development inputs, although there is large amount of variation among the different inputs in terms of their utilization.

In order to understand the variation that existed in the utilization of the various inputs, we have chosen three major types of development inputs, viz., (i) distribution of *patta* land, (ii) utilization of the financial assistance in house building, and (iii) distribution of solar cells in the three blocks.

Table 18 A. Utilization of Development inputs among the Lodhas of three administrative blocks

Sl. No	Name of Development inputs	Number of Beneficiary who received the inputs	Utilized the Development inputs	Could not utilize the Development inputs
1	Patta Land given by Government	(3.26)45[7.95]	(1.95)27	(1.30)18
2	Land given by NGO	(0.72)10[1.77]	(0.51)07	(0.22)03
3	House	(12.66)175[30.92]	(7.38)102	(5.28)73
4	Job card	(8.32)115[20.32]	(6.22)86	(2.10)29
5	Pond	(0.29)04[0.71]	(0.29)04	00
6	Money for domestic animal	(1.01)14[2.47]	(1.01)14	00
7	Training for skill development	(0.43)06[1.06]		(0.43)06
8	Husking Machine & Spray Machine	(0.79)11[1.94]	(0.79)11	00
9	Loan(MT & Babui Cultivation)	(2.46)34[6.01]	(1.09)15	(1.37)19
10	Old age Pension	(1.16)16[2.83]	(1.16)16	00
11	Solar	(7.60)105[18.55]	(4.63)64	(2.97)41
12	Cattle	(1.95)27[4.77]	(1.23)17	(0.73)10
13	Blanket	(0.29)04[0.71]	(0.29)04	00
Total		**(40.95)566[100.00]**	**(26.56)373[64.84]**	**(14.40)199[35.16]**

[ ] Figures in parentheses represent percentages out of the total household's beneficiaries.
( ) Figures in parentheses represent percentages out of the total population.

Table 18 B. Profiles of Development inputs received by the Lodha families in the study area

Only House/ House building loan	House, patta & Solar	House & Patta land	House & Solar cell	Cattle & house	Only Solar	Only Patta	Loan	Old age pension	Job card	Money for domestic animal	Husking & spray machine	Total
52 (12.94)	17 (4.23)	22 (5.47)	57 (14.18)	27 (6.72)	31 (7.71	06 (1.49)	34 (8.46)	16 (3.98)	115 (28.61)	14 (3.48)	11 (2.74)	402 [29.09]

[ ] Represents percentages out of the total population. ( ) Represents percentages out of the total number of beneficiaries.

Note: Four persons received pond, six people given skill development training and ten persons received land from NGO in Daharpur village of Narayangarh block and four persons received blanket in Binpur-II block.

Table 19. Utilization of Patta Land by the Lodhas in the three Blocks (Appendix 1)

Total no. of households	No. of households who received patta	No. of households utilising the patta land	No. of households who received the patta but could not utilise the land
332	45 (13.55)	27(8.13)[60.00]	18(5.42)[40.00]

( ) Figures in parentheses represent percentages out of the total number of households.

[ ] Figures in parentheses represent percentages out of the total Patta holder.

Table 19 shows that only forty five households (13.55%) received *patta* land out of three hundred thirty two households but 8.13 percent beneficiary families utilised the *patta* land out of the total number of households, whereas 5.42 percent beneficiaries could not utilise the *patta* land. In course of our fieldwork, we have found two major factors behind the non-utilization of *patta* land by the beneficiary families, viz., (i) in a number of cases it was found that the *patta* holder has received the official papers but could not cultivate it since the land is being utilised by members of other powerful and dominant communities, and (ii) the *patta* holder is not being able to cultivate the land owing to lack of agricultural implements, irrigation facilities and training. The following cases may illustrate the situation. The names in the case studies have been changed.

Box I

Case Study 1

Name of informant: Tapan Sabar Age: 44 Sex: Male
Village: Amlasole, JL. No: 25 Block: Binpur-II

According to the respondent there are six members in his family. They are dependent on forest resource collection and daily labour. He had received a record of right on *patta* land from the Block Land and Land Reforms Department in 2004. The family had also received financial assistance for house building in 2004. All the family members were living in the house but it was not suitable for living as the roof got damaged. Tapan said: 'Our house is in a very poor condition because it was built by bricks with mud and thatched by tin with a single door made by plain sheet of tin and there is neither any window nor any ventilation system. The house was constructed by a contractor under the supervision of some Government official and they did not consult us regarding the planning of the house. Moreover, if the house requires repair we will not be able to do it without the help of the contractors who made the construction.' Jiban also added: 'I have received *patta* land on paper in 2004 and the amount of the land is 0.15 acre only, but till now I have not seen the land or the plot which has been allotted under my name. May be some other person is cultivating the land. The Government official who gave the *patta* paper to me did not show the actual spot where my piece of land is located'. (Panda and Guha, 2014)

Box II

Case Study 2

Name of informant: Amal Bhakta Age: 48 Sex: Male
Village: Singdhui, JL. No: 25 Block: Nayagram

According to Amal Bhakta there are four members in his family. They are dependent on forest resource collection and cultivation for their survival. The informant received 0.82 acres of *patta* land with record from the Government in 2003. Amal has also received 2 acres of land for Babui grass cultivation in 1981 and solar cell in 2002. He said: 'I have received *patta* land and cultivating it since 2005 and I had cultivated the Babui cultivation land only twice since I received the land.' He added: 'I received *patta* land with record in 2003, but I started cultivation on the land in 2005 because I could not procure plough and bullocks for agriculture. I still do not have those necessary items but I have been able to hire them from my neighbours in exchange of money. But the problem is I do not get those items on hire in every agricultural season. So I could not cultivate the *patta* and *babui* land every year.' He also stated: 'I think the Government should give bullocks and plough to those beneficiaries w ho have no agricultural implement and bullock'.

Box III

Case Study 3

Name of informant: Sambhu Sabar Age: 42 Sex: Male
Village: Amlasole, JL. No: 25 Block: Binpur-II

According to Sambhu they are dependent on forest product collection and daily labour for their survival. The informant received (i) *patta* land from the Block Land and Land Reforms (BLLRO) Department, (ii) financial assistance for house building under IAY scheme from the Government and (iii) domestic animal from Panchayat Department in 2005. He narrated: 'I have received the papers on *patta* land in 06.12.2005. The plot nos. 206 and 203 in the Amlasole *mouza* were allotted to me and the total amount of the land was 0.60 acre only, but till now I could not cultivate the land.' According to him: 'The patta was issued in favour of my father late Samba Sabar. But I could not cultivate these lands because a man belonging to the Mahata Community was cultivating the land and he did not want to forgo his rights.'

I complained the matter to the BLLRO but the Government officials told me that the *patta* land should have been transferred under my name after the death of my father and only after that I may be able to cultivate in the land.' Sambhu reported about the financial assistance given to him for building his house.
Sanbhu continued: 'The newly built house was not suitable for living and I am still living in my old ancestral house and use the new house for keeping the minor forest products and the domestic animals. This is due to the poor planning of the house by the contractor appointed by the panchayats who did not care to consult us.' He further added: 'I also received six goats in 2005 but after thirteen days all the goats died because the goats were not vaccinated and the they were also very weak. Moreover, I have not been provided with any training regarding the rearing and proper upkeep of the domestic animals.'

The financial assistance for the construction of house presented a better scenario than distribution of *patta* land to the Lodhas. A little more than half of the total number of beneficiary families received financial assistance for house building. But what is interesting is the percentage of full utilization of this development input. About thirty percent of the families have fully utilised the aforesaid financial assistance while twenty two percent of the households could not use the financial help properly. The major reason behind the non-utilization of constructed houses lay in poor and non-participatory nature of planning towards the construction of the houses by the concerned department of the Government. In most of the cases, the houses in which the Lodhas were found to live properly were being planned in a participatory manner. In those cases, the financial assistance were given directly to the beneficiary families either by the Government officials or by some NGOs and the beneficiary families were given the liberty to plan and construct the houses according to their needs and demand. The cases described above (Case 1 and 3) illustrate the contrasting nature of the utilization of the financial assistance by the beneficiaries and also the role of the development managers (Table 20).

The solar cells were distributed to the Lodha beneficiaries in the study area under the RSVY scheme for using them for domestic purpose. We have found that at the time of our fieldwork out of 105 families sixty four were found to use the solar powered cells to glow lamps in their house but at the same time it was also found that about 39.05 percent of the families have either sold them at a low price or those gadgets were lying non-functional. Solar plates containing very costly batteries required good maintenance and none of the beneficiary families who were given this sophisticated gadget had undergone any training as regards their maintenance.

Moreover, since the Lodha families were very poor and were badly in need for cash for their daily subsistence, sale of these solar cells served them very well.

Many of the Lodha beneficiaries reported to us that these solar cells fetched them a good amount of money, since their well-to-do Santal and Mahata neighbours were ready to purchase those gadgets. We present below some representative case studies on the use and non-utilization of solar cells by the Lodha families in our study area (Table 21).

Table 23 shows that the highest percentage of families of the Nayagram block received financial assistance from the Government to build their houses and the lowest percentage was found among the Lodhas of Narayangarh.But the financial assistance towards house building was best utilised by the Lodhas of Narayangarh indicating better level of consciousness of the beneficiaries.

Table 20. Utilization of house construction by the Lodhas in the three Blocks

Total no. of households	No. of households who received financial assistance for house construction	No. of households who fully utilised the financial assistance for house construction	No. of households who received financial assistance for house construction b ut could not use it properly.
332	175 (52.71)	102 [58.29] (30.72)	73[41.71] (21.99)

( ) Figures in parentheses represent percentages out of the total number of households.
[ ] Figures in parentheses represent percentages out of the total household's beneficiaries.

Table 21. Utilization of Solar Cell by the Lodhas in the three Blocks

Total no. of households	No. of households who received Solar plate	No. of households fully utilising Solar plate	No. of households who received the solar plate but after few days they have either sold the Solar plate or those became non-functional
332	105 (32.63)	64[60.95](19.28)	41[39.05](12.35)

( ) Figures in parentheses represent percentages out of the total number of households.
[ ] Figures in parentheses represent percentages out of the total household's beneficiaries

BOX IV

Case Study 4

Name of informant: Madhu Sabar Age: 43 Sex: Male
Village: Chirakuti, JL. No: 91 Block: Binpur-II

According to Madhu Sabar there are four members in his family. The family did not possess any agricultural land and no *patta* was given to this family by the Government. They were fully depended on minor forest produce collection for survival. Madhu told that he was not a member of the Forest Protection Committee under the Joint Forest Management programme of the forest department. He received a solar cell in 2004 from the Government under the RSVY scheme although he had to deposit Rs. 500/- to the Panchayat Pradhan (Head) for receiving the solar cell. No money receipt was given to him. Madhu did not think that it was illegal. He frankly admitted, 'Once I received the solar cell, I decided to sell it. After a few days, two men came to me from Ghatshila of the neighbouring Jharkhand state and wanted to buy the cell. I agreed to sell it at a price of Rs. 1000/-. Then there was a bargain and finally I sold it at a price of Rs.700/- since I was badly in need of some money. Already I deposited Rs.500/- to the Panchayat Pradhan.'

Madhu further added 'I sold this gadget because it had no use for a poor man like me. My net gain was Rs.200/- and still I was happy because I decided to purchase some utensils which was more useful for the family and I was looking for the money since long.' However, when I pointed out that the actual price of the solar cell was between Rs. 8000/- to Rs.10, 000/-, Madhu was really surprised. In fact, he had no idea about its price, since nobody told him about the market price of the gadget and the Government officials did not give him any training for using the gadget.

In Nayagram also the scenario of uitilisation was found to be fairly good whereas the utilization percentage at Binpur II was found to be very poor (case study nos. 1 and 5). Examples of successful utilization of financial assistance towards house building are narrated as contrasting case studies from Nayagram and Narayangarh (case study nos. 6 and 7).

Box V

Case Study 5

Name of informant: Swapan Mallick Age: 52 Sex: Male
Village: Singdhui, JL. No: 06 Block: Nayagram

According to Swapan they are dependants on forest resource collection and daily labour for their survival.

He received a solar cell in 2004 under the RSVY scheme and financial assistance for house building in 1994 under IAY scheme from the Government Swapan said: 'I received the solar cell in 2004 and for this I had to deposit Rs. 1200/- to the Panchayat Pradhan in 2003. After receiving the solar cell, I used it for lighting bulbs in my house. After few days in this year in the summer, I could not get any work as daily labour and during this period the forest was also dry. It was a period of acute crisis. So I decided to sell the solar cell for sheer survival. I talked to a well-to-do Mahata family of Chandabila village of Nayagram block through my father-in-law that I wanted to sell my solar cell. After three days the man came to my home with a CPI (M) leader and asked me about the price of the solar cell. I replied to him that it will be Rs. 8000/-. After hearing the rate the leader said to me, 'You don't know the real price of the solar cell in the market. But I did not want to keep down my price. Next day, a man came to my home by riding on a motorcycle. His name was Bijoy Mahata. He came from Singaduba village. I sold it to him at a price of Rs. 6000/- and with the money I purchased a bicycle, some clothes for my family members and repaired my house. I was in need for these things more than the solar cell.'

He added: 'I have no money in my hand to purchase food items like rice, wheat and oil etc. even from the Public Distribution Shop in which those items were sold at a lower price than the market.' Swapan again stated: 'I received financial assistance for house building in 1994 but the newly built house was not suitable for living. The construction a nd plan of the house was very poor since it was made by the Government contractor who did not consult me. Had we built the house by following our traditional methods and raw materials, it would have been much better for us to live in it.'

Table 22. Profiles of patta records and cultivation on patta land among the Lodha/ Sabar Householdsin Binpur-II, Nayagram & Narayangarh Blocks of Paschim (west) Medinipur

Surveyed Households				**No. of Households who received patta record**				**No. of Households found to be actually cultivating patta land**			
Binpur II	Nayagram	Narayangarh	Total	Binpur II	Nayagram	Narayangarh	Total	Binpur II	Nayagram	Narayangarh	Total
87	182	63	332	10 [11.94] (3.01)	28 [15.38] (8.43)	17 [26.98] (5.12)	45 [13.55] (13.55)	01 [10.00] (0.30)	11 [39.28] (3.31)	15 [88.28] (4.51)	27 [60.00] (8.13)

( ) Figures in parentheses represent percentages out of the total number of households.

[ ] Figures in parentheses represent percentages out of the block wise patta holder.

The above table shows the scenario of *patta* land distribution by the Government and its utilisation by the Lodha families in the three blocks of the study area. It is found that the condition of the Binpur-II block is worst both in terms of *patta* distribution and its utilisation by the beneficiary families. About twelve percent of the total number of surveyed households received *patta* land from the Government and only one family was found to use it whereas, in Narayangarh twenty seven percent of the total number of families received *patta* land and as high as eighty eight percent of the families were found to cultivate their land. In Nayagram the percentage of recipients was about fifteen, while the users turned out to be thirty nine percent.

Table 23. Profiles of Houshing scheme distribution and used under Indira Awas Yojana and Lodhs housing scheme among the Lodha/ Sabar Households in Binpur-II, Nayagram & Narayangarh Blocks of Paschim (west) Medinipur

Surveyed Households				**No. of Households who received financial assistance under the scheme**				**No. of Households who actually utilised the benefits of the scheme**			
Binpur -II	Nayagram	Narayan garh	Total	Binpur - II	Nayagram	Narayan garh	Total	Binpur -II	Nayagram	Narayan garh	Total
87	182	63	332	36 [41.37] (10.84)	124 [68.13] (37.35)	15 [23.81] (4.52)	175 (52.71)	12 [33.33] (3.61)	75 [60.48] (22.59)	15 [100.00] (4.52)	102 [58.29] (30.72)

( ) Figures in parentheses represent percentages out of the total number of households.

[ ] Figures in parentheses represent percentages out of the block wise patta holder.

From the above table it is found that the highest percentage of families of the Nayagram block received financial assistance from the Government to build their houses and the lowest percentage was found among the Lodhas of Narayangarh.But the financial assistance towards house building was best utilised by the Lodhas of Narayangarh indicating higher level of consciousness of the beneficiaries. In Nayagram also the scenario of uitilisation was found to be fairly good whereas the utilisation percentage at Binpur II was found to be very poor (case study nos. 1 and 5). Examples of successful utilisation of financial assistance towards house building are narrated as contrasting case studies from Nayagram and Narayangarh (case study nos. 6 and 7).

Table 24. Profiles of Solar cell distribution and Utilization among the Lodha/Sabar Households in Binpur II, Nayagram & Narayangarh Blocks of Paschim (west) Medinipur

Surveyed Households				**No. of Households who received Solar Plate**				**No. of Households found to be actually use the Solar plate**			
Binpur II	Nayagram	Narayangarh	Total	Binpur II	Nayagram	Narayangarh	Total	Binpur II	Nayagram	Narayangarh	Total
87	182	63	332	23 [26.64] (6.92)	82 [45.05] (24.69)	Nil	105 (32.63)	04 [17.39] (1.20)	60 [73.17] (18.07)	Nil	64 [60.95] (19.28)

( ) Figures in parentheses represent percentages out of the total number of households.

[ ] Figures in parentheses represent percentages out of the block wise patta holder.

The distribution of solar cells by the Government was done in Binpur-II and Nayagram. The Lodha families of Narayangarh block were not covered under this scheme. Our respondents of Narayangarh reported that according to Government officials, the families of this block were considered to be in a better economic condition so they were not provided with solar cells. The percentage of families who received solar cells was much higher in Nayagram and we have also found better utilisation of this gadget in this block. In Binpur-II only four families out of twenty three were found to use solar cells. Most of the families in Binpur II were found to have sold out the solar cells at very low price to outsiders in order to meet their domestic needs (case study nos. 2 and 3).

Box VI

Case Study 6

Name of informant: Ganesh Bhakta Age: 55 Sex: Male
Village: Bansiasole JL. No: 06 Block: Nayagram

Ganesh Bhakta lives in a joint family. His old parents reside with him. He has one daughter and a son. His brother and brother's wife and son also share the same household. Formerly they were dependant on forest product collection and daily labour. In 1993, Ganesh received about 0.82 acres of *patta* land with record of right from the Block Land and Land Reforms (BLLRO) Department and he has been cultivating paddy in the land. Only one crop is grown in this land since there is no irrigation facility. According to Ganesh: 'I have received *patta* land and cultivating it since 1994 with the help of my family members. In the early stage, I could not procure plough and bullocks, but I have been able to hire them from my neighbours in exchange of money. In 1999, I bought a pair of bullocks. I earned the money by selling paddy grown in my land. Then I also bought a plough. Since 2000, I have been able to cultivate my *patta* land in every agricultural season.' Being encouraged in agriculture he purchased 0.10 acre of agricultural land from a Mahata farmer of nearby Malam village. Ganesh received financial assistance for house building under IAY scheme in 2004 from the Government. He said: 'After receiving financial assistance for house building in 2004 I made my house according to my plan and employed some members of my own community for the construction of the house. The officers of the Government department came to inspect my house and they were satisfied. I am now living comfortably in my house.' Ganesh also received old age pension for his parents in 2005, which is Rs.750/- per month. He received the pension money twice in a year from the local post office and according to him: 'The cash m oney helps us to cover a lot of expenses for my large family.'(Panda and Guha, 2012).

Box VII

Case Study 7

Name of informant: Biswanath Kotal Age: 45 Sex: Male
Village: Daharpur Block: Narayangarh

Biswanath Kotal lives in a joint family with his old father, wife, two sons and an unmarried brother. They are dependent on daily labour and cultivation for their survival. Biswanath works as a truck driver although it is his secondary occupation. He received various types of development inputs such as:

(i) financial assistance for house building under IAY scheme in 2009 from the Government, (ii) pond for Pisciculture in 2010 from the Panchayat Department, (iii) job card in 2008 from Panchayat Department, (iv) money for the purchase of domestic animal in 2010 from Self-Help-Group (SHG), (v) skill development training in 2010 from Panchayat Department, and (vi) loan in 2010 from SHG. He said: 'I have received an amount of Rs.35,000/- as financial assistance for house building in 2004 and I am living in this house very comfortably since the house was made according to our plan and constructed by a Lodha mason whom I employed from a different village. The house was constructed with cement and bricks and thatched with asbestos. I had to spend an additional amount of Rs.15, 000/-.towards the construction of the house. I earned the money by working as truck driver. In the same year the Government department gave me monetary help to dig a pond on at the vicinity of my house in my land for Pisciculture'. Biswanath, however, could not start pisciculture in the pond since he thought that the pond was still not ready for the purpose. He used the pond for domestic purposes, like bathing and washing of clothes and utensils. The water of the pond was used by him for the construction of his house. According to him: 'I will continue to use the pond for the domestic purpose and after five years I will start Pisciculture'. He further added: 'My wife is an active member of the village self-help-group and she has received Rs. 5000/- as loan and we have purchased a cow and four goats with this money from the *hat (weekly market)*. After one month, the goats died because we lacked the necessary training for rearing the goats.' He received training for mushroom cultivation for three days which was organised by the Gram Panchayat and after the training, he received one pack of mushroom seed for cultivation, although he did not cultivate mushroom because he could not find a suitable place of mushroom cultivation in his house.

Chapter V

The Comparative Scenario of the Utilization of the Development Inputs

In this section, we have made an attempt to compare the utilization pattern of the four major development inputs given to the Lodhas in the study area which contains three blocks of the Paschim Medinipur district. The rationale behind the comparison is twofold. Firstly, through this comparison we have presented the overall scenario of the utilization vis-à-vis non-utilization of the development inputs by the study population at a glance.

Secondly, the comparison also revealed the variation among the households in the three blocks as regards the utilization of the development inputs.

In table 25, we have made an overall assessment of the utilization of five kinds of development inputs provided by the Government to the Lodha families of three blocks of the study area. Besides the distribution of *patta* land, financial assistance for house building and solar cells, we have included distribution of job card under the MGNREGA and cattle, in this overall assessment.

It would be interesting to look at the non-utilization and/or partial utilization of the five kinds of development inputs by the beneficiaries of the three blocks who received the inputs from the Government. The beneficiaries of Binpur II were found to be lagging much behind the beneficiaries of the other two blocks as regards the utilization of *patta* land, solar cells, house building and cattle rearing loans.

Table 25. The Major Development inputs and block wise utilization and non-utilization among the Lodhas

Name of the Block	Development Inputs	No. of households who received inputs	No. of households who fully utilised the inputs	No. of households who received the inputs but could not use or partially used them
Binpur-II	Solar Cell	23	(1.37)04 [17.39]	19 [82.61]
	Patta Land	10	(0.34)01 [10.00]	09 [90.00]
	House	36	(4.10)12 [33.33]	24 [66.67]
	Cattle	25	(1.71)05 [20.00]	20 [80.00]
	Jobcard	23	(6.83)20 [86.96]	03 [13.04]
Nayagram	Solar Cell	82	(20.48)60 [73.17]	22 [26.83]
	Patta Land	28	(3.75)11 [39.29]	17 [60.71]
	House	124	(25.60) 75 [60.48]	49 [39.52]
	Cattle	02		02 [100.00]
	Jobcard	50	(12.29)36 [72.00]	14 [28.00]
Narayangarh	Solar Cell	Nil		
	Patta Land	17	(5.12)15 [88.28]	02 [11.72]
	House	15	(5.12)15 [100.00]	Nil
	Cattle	14	(3.07)09 [64.29]	05 [35.71]
	Jobcard	42	(10.24)30 [71.43]	12 [28.57]
Total		**491**	**293**	**198**

[ ] Figures in parentheses represent percentages out of the total household's beneficiaries.

( ) Figures in parentheses represent percentages out of the column total.

The success rate of beneficiaries towards the utilization of the *patta* land, house building and cattle rearing was found to be highest at Narayangarh among the three blocks. The distribution of cattle and poultry birds among the Lodhas of our survey population also revealed that the beneficiaries could not manage their cattle and birds owing to lack of basic knowledge in rearing the animals. As a result, we have found that many cattle, particularly goats, have died in a short span of time after those were given to the beneficiaries. Nayagram beneficiaries were found to occupy the middle position between Binpur II and Narayangarh. The highest percentage of job card was found to be used by the Lodha families of Binpur II which indicated their poor economic condition. Only thirteen percent of the Lodha families did not use the job card. The percentages of non-utilization of job card by the Lodha families of Nayagarm and Narayangarh were 28 and 28.57 respectively.

Block -Wise Description of the Utilization of the Major Development Inputs

Binpur II Block

Land Distribution

In this block we have found that land *pattas* were issued and given to the Lodha beneficiary families with records but the ground reality was that the beneficiaries had not seen the plot, let alone cultivated the allotted land. In all the cases, *pattas* were issued during 1985-89 but except one none of the *patta* holders were found to cultivate their land. These lands were vest land, i.e., they were owned by the Government on paper but were being cultivated by the members of the numerically and politically dominant communities of the region, viz. Santals and Mahatas. The Government land department issued *patta* to the Lodha families without enquiring into this important fact. After the issuance of the *patta* it was not possible for the marginalised Lodha families to claim their rights over these lands given to them by the Government. Till date, the Lodhas did not have any knowledge about their proper right on received *patta* record. The Land and Land Reforms Department officials have not also given any guidance to the beneficiary families about the location of the land. In this block *patta* land was received by ten beneficiary families but the real scenario was only one beneficiary family was found to cultivate the land. This piece of land was actually purchased from a Mahata family by the Government and subsequently given to the Lodha family. So, in this particular case the land could be utilised by the beneficiary.

House Construction

Lodhas got houses under Indira Awas Yojana (IAY) scheme, which were constructed by contractors employed by the concerned Government department. But the houses, in most of the cases, were not suitable for living. Because, in the house there was no window in the room and the beneficiaries were also found to live in a single room with goat, cow, hen etc. In this block, thirty six families, i.e., 10.84 percent of the total, received houses out of eighty seven households. Actually, only twelve beneficiary families (33.33%) used the house comfortably and twenty four families (66.67%) could not use the house properly.

Distribution of Solar Cell

In this block, the Lodhas received solar cells as a development input from the Government. But they had no idea or knowledge about how to use this high technology gadget. After receiving the solar cells they were very glad but whenever they fell into economic crisis they sold the solar cell to the wealthy neighbours at a very cheap price ranging between. Rs.3000 - Rs5000 only. The then market price of solar cell was around Rs.25000/-. Only twenty families received solar cell out of eighty seven, but only four families (17.39%) used the solar cells and nineteen families (82.61%) sold it to the wealthy neighbours.

An informant of Tildahi village told 'Till five years ago, villagers had to travel fifteen kilometers to buy salt and cooking oil, and the nearest high school was in Belpahari – about 23 kilometers away.' A Lodha informant said 'We are hungrier than the other Lodhas of this block because we have no homestead or agricultural land and could not get sufficient food twice daily'.

Cattle

In this block, the Lodhas received cattle (goats, pigs and cows) and poultry birds as development inputs several times from the Government but these animals were neither vaccinated nor were the beneficiaries given any training on the proper rearing of the animals by the concerned department of the Government. As a result, in most of the cases the animals died within one month. According to the beneficiaries, there was no suitable place in their house to keep the cattle.

Nayagram Block

Land Distribution

In this block, it was found that land *pattas* were issued and given to the Lodha beneficiary families but the real truth is 39. 29 percent beneficiaries utilised the *patta* land for cultivation whereas 60.71 percent beneficiaries were unable to cultivate the land because these Lodhas had no bullock and plough or agricultural implements and they did not have sufficient money to hire the bullock and plough. The land which was received from the Government was all high land (*Danga Jami*). So, the land could not be cultivated which was allotted to the beneficiaries.

House Construction

Lodhas received houses under Indira Awas Yojana (IAY) and Rastriya Sama Vikas Yojana (RSVY) schemes, which were made by Government department but houses were not suitable for living. Because in the house there was no window in the room, they were also found to live in a single room with goat, cow, hen etc. In these block 124 families (68.13%) received houses out of 182 but seventy five families (60.48%) used the house comfortably and forty nine families (39.51%) could not use the house properly. In this block some houses were constructed by one NGO with the help of the Government. The condition of these houses was better than those constructed by the contractors employed by the Government. It was reported by the informants that the representatives of the NGO consulted with the owner of the houses before the construction. This kind of scenario as regards the utilization of financial assistance towards house building was not found in the Binpur II block.

Distribution of Solar Cell

In this block, eighty two beneficiary families (45.05%) received solar cells out of 182 families and sixty beneficiary families (73.17%) used this high technology gadget whereas twenty two beneficiary families (26.83%) have sold the solar cells to the wealthy neighbours because they did not know how to use the solar cell. The scenario was much better than the Lodhas of the Binpur II block. The successful user of solar cell among the Lodhas learnt about the proper use of this technology from the neighbouring higher caste families.

Cattle

In this block, it was found that only two families received goats from the Government and the animals died after a few days. Here also the lack of training regarding the rearing of the domestic animals among the beneficiaries seemed to be the cause behind the death of the animals.

Narayangarh Block

Land Distribution

Here we have found that more than eighty eight percent of the beneficiary families were cultivating their *patta* land given by the Government, although they did not possess plough, bullocks and other agricultural implements. They were found to hire those implements from the neighbouring villages in order to cultivate their lands given by the Government and it was also reported by a number of informants that they could not perform agriculture in the *patta* land since they did not get implements and bullocks every year on hire.

In the seventies, cultivable and homestead land were given to some Lodha families by an NGO named the *Institute of Social Research and Applied Anthropology* (ISRAA) which was founded by late Professor Probodh Kumar Bhowmick of the University of Calcutta with a mission to conduct applied anthropological research and development work among the Lodhas of the region. The Institute organised agriculture training for the Lodhas, although the organization could not provide them agricultural implements owing to paucity of funds.

House Construction

In this block the Lodhas received money to build their houses under Indira Awas Yojna (IAY). The houses were made by their own planning. So, those who have received house building loan have been living in the house comfortably. Here fifteen beneficiary families (23.81%) received house construction loans out of sixty three and all the houses were found to be in a much better condition than the houses in the other two blocks in our study area.

Notably, in Narayngarh block, we have found six Self-Help-Groups (SHG) constituted by the Lodhas. All the groups were found to be active. The SHGs were formed by the initiative of the Lodha women and the SHG members reported that they did not receive any kind of help and cooperation from the Gram Panchayat and the local leadership of the CPI (M) towards the formation and the running of the SHGs. Some of the SHG women reported that they received various kinds of skill development training organised by the panchayat but they were not given any material input by the Government so that they could apply their knowledge and skill in income generating activities. Solar cell s were not given to the Lodha families of this block.

Distribution of Cattle

Unlike Binpur II and Nayagram, here the beneficiaries received financial assistance to purchase domestic animals from the Government through the SHG. So, the beneficiaries purchased the cows and goats by their own choice and initiative. Some of the beneficiaries purchased the animals from neighbouring villagers while others bought them in the local market (*hat*). The goats and cows purchased from the local market however, died early.

In sum, fourteen beneficiary households received financial assistance for purchasing domestic animals from the Government and nine families were successful in rearing the cattle while in case of five families the animals died after one month. According to the beneficiaries, some SHG members received training from the personnel of the Animal Husbandry Department of the Block Office organized by the local Gram Panchayat.

Table 26. Comparative Scenario of the Utilization of Major Development inputs among the Lodha Households in three blocks of Paschim (west) Medinipur

Develop-ment Inputs	Binpur-II		Nayagram		Narayangarh	
	Utilised	Unutilised	Utilised	Unutilised	Utilised	Unutilised
Solar cell	04[17.39]	19[82.61]	60[73.17]	22[26.83]	Solar cell has not been given.	
Patta Land	01[10.00]	09[90.00]	11[39.29]	17[60.71]	15[88.28]	02[11.72]
House	12[33.33]	24[66.67]	75[60.48]	49[39.52]	15[100.00]	00
Cattle	05[20.00]	20[80.00]	00	02[100.00]	09[64.29]	05[35.71]
Total	**22(23.40)**	**72(76.60)**	**146 (61.86)**	**90(38.14)**	**39(84.78)**	**07(15.22)**

[ ] Represents the number of households out of the total beneficiary households in a particular block for a specific development input

( ) Represents the number of households out of the total beneficiary households in a particular block for all development inputs.

The comparative scenario of the utilization of the four major development inputs in the three blocks among the Lodhas showed a marked overall variation. Variation is also found in terms of the type of development input. Let us first enumerate the variations.

1. The development inputs given to the Lodhas have been utilised by them most successfully in the Narayangarh block and interestingly, solar plates have not been given at all in this block.
2. The worst scenario is found in the Binpur II block in which non-utilization of all the development inputs predominated the scene. Nayagram lies in the middle position in terms of the utilization of the development inputs.
3. When we look separately to each development input, we find that the utilization of domestic cattle can be regarded as a kind of

development input which turned out to be an unutilised one except among the Lodhas of Narayangarh who showed the best performance in the utilization of all the inputs.

4. The utilization of financial assistance for house construction given as a development input showed that even the overall worst performers (Lodhas of Binpur-II) have made a substantial utilization of house construction as a development input.
5. Regarding *patta* land, we do not find full utilization in any of the blocks studied but in case of house we find full utilization in Narayangarh Block.
6. The development assistance given in the form of cattle revealed a grim scenario both at Binpur II and Nayagram blocks while the performance of the beneficiaries towards the utilization of this input was found to be fairly well in Narayangarh block.

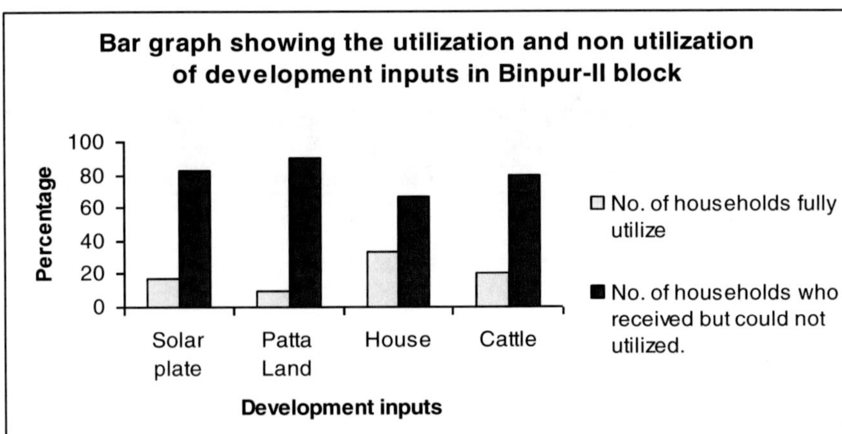

Figure 11. Bar graph showing the utilization and non utilization of development inputs in Binpur II block.

A Closer Look at Daharpur Village of the Narayangarh Block

The comparative scenario of development described in the previous section revealed that the Lodhas of Narayangarh block achieved the best utilization of the inputs to improve their livelihood opportunities. We may recall here that we have studied only one village named Daharpur in this administrative block. In fact the total population of the Daharpur village is 343 which is almost equal to the population of the villages of Nayagram and Binpur II blocks when each of them is considered separately. In order to look into the reasons behind the success of the Lodhas in the Daharpur village, which represents the Narayangarh block in our sample we have studied the scenario of development in this village in some detail in a diachronic frame of reference. Let us get into the detail.

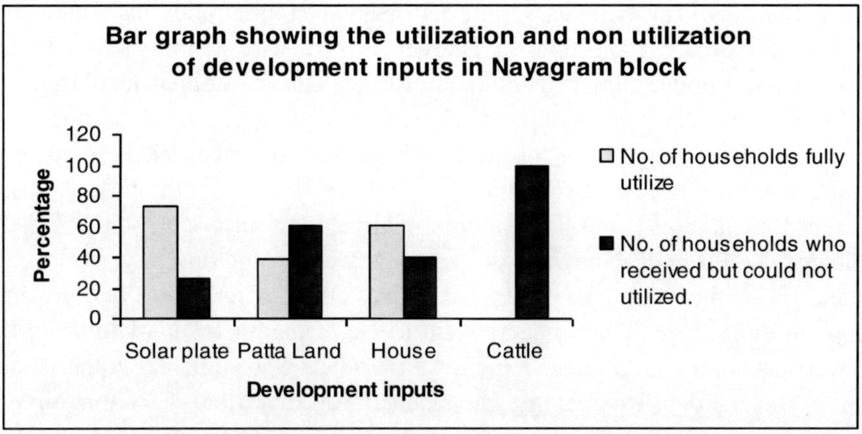

Figure 12. Bar graph showing the utilization and non utilization of development inputs in Nayagram block.

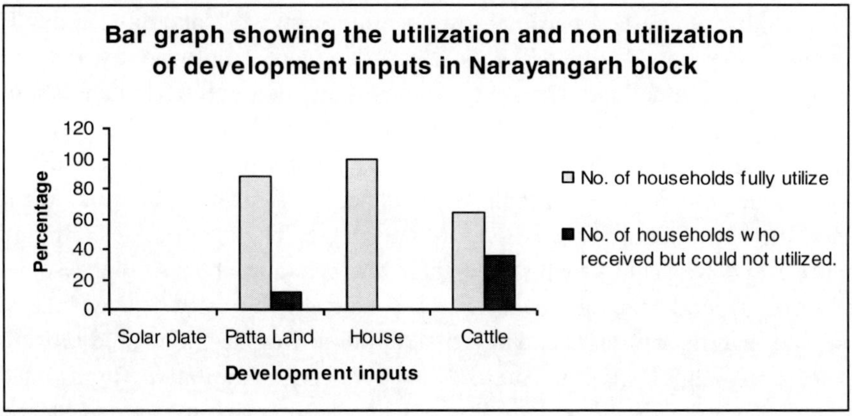

Figure 13. Bar graph showing the utilization and non utilization of development inputs in Narayangarh block.

Ethnographic Description of the Daharpur Village

An ethnographic description of the Daharpur village is found in an article of Probodh Kumar Bhowmick published in the 1961 District Census Handbook, Midnapore. According to Bhowmick Daharpur was a multi-ethnic village and in the Mughal period, there was no tribal people in the village. Most of the area was covered by the dense forest and thorny bamboo groves. The population consisted of a few scheduled castes and one or two clean castes families. The Munda, Lodha and Santal communities have migrated later in this area. At the time of Bhowmick's fieldwork, only seven Lodha families lived in the village. The Santal, Munda and the Lodhas lived together and maintained their separate cultural identity distinguishable from the caste groups. There was a free primary school run by two teachers, a club established in 1960, and a *Siva* temple; a village fair was held on the last day of the Bengali year and the *Charak* festival was also celebrated by the villagers. In Probodh Bhowmick's account, we did not find any report of a Lodha girl or boy going to the free primary school. There were two grocer's shops in the village. The villagers went to Narayangarh for marketing. In the Late fifties, a rehabilitation scheme for the Lodhas was launched in the village and a social education centre was opened for the tribals. At that time a community grain-bank (*Gola*) to facilitate paddy loans to the tribal was also established by the Tribal Welfare Department of the Government of West Bengal. According to Bhowmick, in this village there were many caste-specific hereditary occupations like cultivation, tending cattle, cleaning and drying cloths, umbrella repairing, drum beating, iron work and day labour. The Lodhas, being outside the Hindu caste order were employed by the clean castes as whole-time labourers on annual contract although no female labourer of the Lodhas were employed. The higher castes had all the landed property and they did not plough or even performed manual labour. For agricultural purpose, they employed the tribals as permanent or seasonal labourers. In early period the caste hierarchy was seen in the village. The clean castes (Brahmin, Sadgope and Kayastha) maintained their higher status in the village society. Bhowmick found that the social scenario had already started to change and observed that the low caste and the tribal children were found to study together in the same school, although he did not give any quantitative figure on the literacy condition of the village nor did he mention about the school going Lodha children in his village ethnography. He however mentioned that he observed inter-caste participation in religious festivals as well as inter-dinning among the castes. (Bhowmick, 1961:4-47).

In a later period, some social scientists led by Probodh Kumar Bhowmick and his Institute of Social Research and Applied Anthropology (ISRAA) used their own resources and began to function in an adjacent area to establish a colony for the Lodhas at Daharpur in Narayangarh block. The main objectives of the ISRAA relevant for the development of the Lodhas were as follows.

- To give an economic footing to the poverty stricken, landless, nomadic and ex-criminal tribes;
- To socialize them in order to bring them in mainstream of Indian society by inculcating in them the values of the middle class;
- To facilitate the tribal people for their formal and vocational education; (http://www.midnapore.in/museum/bidisa_museum1.html)

With the above objectives ISRAA established a school building, hostel and some education facility were provided to encourage the Lodhas for educating their children. In order to involve the Lodhas to adopt settled agriculture, improved seeds and other inputs were made available to them. A model nursery to supply plants was set up to encourage them in the cultivation of improved varieties of crops. After some years, the school gradually developed from Primary to Secondary level and an adult education centre and a pre-basic nursery school were also opened. In addition to these, family based cottage industries like mat-making, tailoring, weaving, carpentry were started for the self-employment of the Lodhas. Attempts were made to flourish the indigenous cultural resources of the Lodha community through exhibitions and cultural programmes in which the community members performed dance, drama, and songs. These attempts were largely successful. The success of this experiment led to financial assistance from the state Government, although according to Bhowmick, 'new adverse political force s have begun to operate, and are posing new obstacles to this scheme' (Bhowmick, 1981:6-8).

The Present Scenario of Dhaharpur

This village is now under the Gram Panchayat of Makarampur in Narayangar block of Paschim Medinipur district of West Bengal. The village is situated 1 km away from the National Highway 64; it is situated 15 km away from the Midnapore town. The *mouza* name is also Daharpur (J.L. no.26). In this village there are two hamlets locally known as *paras*. One is *Uttar para* (North) in which live the Santal, Munda, Lodhas and the caste Hindu groups while the Paschim Para (West) is inhabited only by the Lodhas.

Most of the villagers are engaged in cultivation as owner cultivators and agricultural labourers.

This village has two primary school s and one high school as well as two Integrated Child Development Scheme (ICDS) centers within its boundary. Each hamlet (*para*) has a primary school and an ICDS centre. There is one High school at Bidisha which was established by Probodh Bhowmick. At present there are two clubs and Siva, Chandi, Kali, Sitala, Hari and Manasa temples. Six grocery shops and five pan(betel leaf) shops are available in the village. But till now there is no market or hat. During field visits the first author did not find any rehabilitation centre and village grain-bank as reported in the ethnographic description of Bhowmick. According to the villagers, the rehabilitation centre became non-functional and its building also collapsed by the year 1985. The Government did not take any initiative to repair or maintain the building. The villagers also told me that the village communal grain-bank continued only for five years. Presently, there were no caste-specific hereditary occupations and the villagers were mainly found to subsist either on cultivation of their own land and agricultural day labourer. Some of them also reported that they migrate as agricultural labourers within and outside the state. In this village, six self-help-groups were found which were constituted by Lodha women in 2005. The literacy percentage of the Lodhas in this village is 71 percent. Drinking water facility is available. In the Lodha *para* there were only two tubewells for drinking water supply and a common big pond for the domestic use of water. The villagers received Job Card from the Block Development Office and were found to use this card for 100 day's work in a year under the Mahatma Gandhi National Rural Employment Guarantee Act (MGNREGA). (Panda, 2012).

Chapter VI

CONCLUSION AND RECOMMENDATIONS

The Lodhas are regarded as a marginalised and economically backward tribe and both the central and the state Government s have allocated funds under various development schemes to improve the socioeconomic condition of the tribe since Independence. The condition of the tribe however did not improve considerably, although, various development inputs were given to this marginalized tribe. The field based studies done by the anthropologists and some voluntary social workers revealed that the Lodhas remained poor and marginalized compared to the any other tribal community in the region where they live with the latter. Under this background, this field based anthropological research has been carried out to make an assessment of the ground realities of the situation regarding the socioeconomic and demographic condition of the Lodhas and also the scenario around the implementation of the development inputs given to them under the governmental schemes in three administrative blocks of Paschim Medinipur district of West Bengal. Anthropological studies on the Lodhas of West Bengal have not yet made any attempt to assess the impact of the development inputs given to this marginalized community from a systematic and quantitative perspective.

In the different chapters of the book, we have made an attempt to assess the utilization of the various developmental inputs given by external agencies (governmental and non-governmental) for the improvement of the Lodhas in the three administrative blocks of Paschim (west) Medinipur district from a quantitative angle. We have also made attempts to compare the development scenario of the Lodhas in the three blocks and finally advanced some recommendations for the all-round socioeconomic development of this poor and marginalized tribe of West Bengal. We now give a brief account of our findings in the following paragraphs.

The Lodhas were included as one among the criminal tribes by the British administration under the Criminal Tribes Act, 1911. In 1952, the Criminal Tribes Act was repealed by the Government and all the communities who were designated as criminal tribes were reclassified as denotified communities. The Lodhas were also included under the denotified and nomadic tribes along with nineteen communities of West Bengal. Still later, since 1971 the Lodhas were designated as one of the Primitive Tribal Groups (PTGs) of India. Lodhas are mainly found in the western part of the state in the districts of Purulia, Bankura and Paschim Medinipur along with tribes like Santal, Munda, Bhumij and Oraon who are numerically and economically in a much better condition than the Lodhas. The Lodhas generally live in and around the forest covered areas of the southwestern districts of the state and still largely depend on forest for their livelihood.

At present the Lodhas do not live exclusively in the forest covered areas, but have spread out in other deforested regions and are found to work there as agricultural and non-agricultural labourers. But their main economy is still based on collection of minor forest products, such as leaves for preparing leaf-plates for sale. According to Bhowmick, the Lodhas were found to collect edible roots and fruits for household consumption and sell the surplus in the local markets. They were also found to be engaged in the collection of tussore cocoons and sell them in the market for cash. Lodhas also catch snakes and lizards and sell their hides and consume the flesh of these animals. They also catch fish and tortoises from the water bodies for domestic consumption as well as for sale. The marginalization of the Lodhas provided a major theme for the anthropologists and the activists in India. But there is hardly any solid empirical village level study which recorded the scenario around the implementation of the development inputs given to this marginalized community. There is also a lack of socio-demographic data on the Lodha community in West Bengal. There exists some data on the nutritional condition of the tribe collected by the biological anthropologists.

It was found that almost all the villages inhabited by the Lodhas in the three blocks were located near forests and suffered from good transport and road condition. In majority of the villages, the Lodha families were found to depend on forest product collection; although, in some villages we have found that agriculture was also being practiced by them. The supply of drinking water facilities, sanitation and health care delivery systems were also found to be in a very poor condition in most of the Lodha villages.

We have described the age -sex composition, sex-ratio, household size, marital status, subsistence pattern and literacy condition among the Lodhas separately in the three blocks and combined these basic socio-demographic data of the three blocks. Our findings showed that the interesting aspect about the demography of the Lodhas in this sample is the preponderance of females in almost all the age groups (the sex ratio being 1100) although longevity of Lodha women was found to be much lower than the men. The greater number of females is most revealing in all the younger age groups from 0-4 up to 35-39.Only in the age groups, 40-44 and 45-49, we find a predominance of males over females.

The marital status showed, the females were found to marry at an early age than the males. But the interesting fact is we have found more unmarried females at higher age groups than the males.

The scenario of the literacy status revealed that the overall literacy condition was not very satisfactory (43.35 %) and the condition of the females in this regard was worse than the males. The percentage of illiterate persons in the early school going age groups (5-14) was higher among the females. The highest number of literate individuals was found among the males in the age group 10-14 while among the females it was in the age group 5-9. When the age categories were combined into larger groups, the literacy condition of the population also revealed that the younger Lodhas had achieved more primary education than the older persons.

The household size of the Lodhas in the surveyed population revealed a predominance of small households ranging between 4-6 persons. The mean household size turned out to be 4.2 persons.

The subsistence pattern of the study area revealed that the Lodhas in the study area were mostly engaged in forest produce collection and they were also found to be working as labourers in the agricultural and non-agricultural sector s. A small number of Lodha families were found to cultivate their own land and a much smaller number were engaged in the service sector.

Subsequently, we have discussed the main empirical findings of the study. Firstly, the governmental perspective towards development inputs among the Lodhas as well as the aim and focus of the RSVY scheme has been discussed. In our study area, we have found that although the chief aim of the Government was to bring the Lodhas into the fold of agriculture and settle them like a group of farmers, the distribution of land by the Land and Land Reforms Department to the landless Lodha families largely remained an unfinished task.

A quantitative analysis of all the development inputs given to the community revealed that 41 percent of the Lodha families in the study received some kind of development inputs from the Government. Our findings further showed that at the time of our survey 402(29.09%) beneficiary families out of 1382 have received various types of developmental inputs in different combinations. The nature of the distribution of developmental inputs by the Government confirmed that emphasis was given to cash loan for house building and high technology solar cells. Through our observation and interviews with the beneficiaries, we have found that most of the houses were built in a hurried manner and seemed to be weak in structure. The beneficiaries also expressed their dissatisfaction with the newly built houses. We have also found that the majority of the beneficiaries who received solar cells either sold them against cash to well-to-do neighbours belonging to other communities or could not use them properly. Any kind of monitoring by the Government as regards the use of such high technology gadget was not observed by us in the field.

Next, the utilization pattern of the three main development inputs, viz., (i) distribution of *patta* land, (ii) financial assistance for house building, and (iii) distribution of solar cells in the three administrative blocks have been narrated in an aggregate manner.

Our findings exposed that a number of the beneficiaries received *patta* land only on paper. Many beneficiaries received financial assistance for house building but in most of the cases the condition of the newly built houses were not suitable for living owing to the poor planning of the house by the contractor appointed by the panchayats who did not care to consult the beneficiaries. A number of beneficiaries received solar cells but they had no knowledge about how to use and maintain the high technology gadgets properly. It was also found that the beneficiaries sold the gadgets to their well-to-do Santal and Mahata neighbours.

We have then described the utilization of the three main development inputs in each block separately and also presented some representative case studies. These case studies were qualitative in nature which brought out the views of the beneficiaries. We have found some variation in the utilization of development inputs in the three blocks. A block-wise description of the five development inputs and their utilization vis-à-vis non-utilization separately has been provided.

Finally, we have provided a comparative scenario of the development inputs in the three administrative blocks. Our findings revealed that the utilization of development inputs was very poor in Binpur II block while those were most successfully utilised in the Narayangarh block. Nayagram lies in the middle position in terms of the utilization of the development inputs.

In this research, we have found micro-level differences in terms of the utilization of development inputs by the Lodha families of the three administrative blocks of Paschim Medinipur district which have a bearing on the macro-level policies undertaken by the Government to ameliorate the socio-economic condition of the most economically disadvantaged and socially marginalized tribal population of a district identified under the macro category named "backward". It was also found that the failure on the part of the Government to make use of the various development inputs to the target group of beneficiaries is related with the specific situation of each block. (Panda and Guha, 2013).

In this work, we have found differences in terms of the utilization of the development inputs by the Lodha families of the three administrative blocks of Paschim Medinipur district. The findings of this research revealed that the Lodha settlement of Binpur II block suffered from poor communication and transport, and lack of access to the political leaders and panchayat members of the area although the local panchayat leader belonged to their own community. The Government has not yet been able to organize skill development programmes for the Lodha women and men of this block.

In Nayagram block, the Lodhas were found to be in better condition than they were in Binpur II, in terms of communication and access to local panchayat leadership. Here the Government had also taken up some programmes through an NGO to monitor the implementation of the development inputs.

In Natrayangarh block, the Lodhas also seemed to be more aware about the development inputs than their counterparts in the other blocks studied in this research. They also owned cultivable land and got training in agriculture and other skill development training programmes organized jointly by an NGO and the state Government.

The Lodhas in Nayagram and Narayangarh blocks were found to inhabit in the vicinity of multi-caste villages and were found to be in good relation with the different caste groups.

Recommendations

Finally, we have made an attempt to enumerate a list of recommendations which may be considered by the concerned departments of the Government and the policymakers for the better implementation of the development inputs according to the specific needs of the Lodha community. In this connection, it may be mentioned that some of the recommendations, which are stated at the end of this book have actually been developed in the impact assessment report submitted to the District Magistrate of Paschim Medinipur in 2006. We would also like to record the fact that the district administration has also adopted some of our recommendations stated in the aforesaid report; a facsimiles of the letter from the District Magistrate and a news item published in *The Statesman* are enclosed under Appendices A and B as supporting documents. Let us enumerate our recommendations.

First, one should identify the ground reality of the poor and economically backward community for the improvement of their socio-economic conditions. Two things should be given utmost priority. The road transport and public communication systems should be improved in all the blocks, particularly in Binpur II and Nayagram. Governmental efforts towards the supply of safe drinking water and minor irrigation systems should be initiated immediately in all the areas inhabited by the Lodhas.

Second, skill development and agricultural training should be given to all the Lodhas of three administrative blocks irrespective of the intra-block variation in terms of population size and distribution. Public Private Partnership (PPP) programme should be attempted to monitor the implementation of the developmental inputs. There are many good NGO's who are already working in the interior regions.

Third, skill development and production of value added items made out of minor forest produce by the Lodha villagers still remained one of the most neglected areas by the Government. The RSVY Plan document also did not give any specific importance to the forest sector which is intimately related to the livelihood of the tribal populations in the "backward districts" of India. In our study area the Lodhas were found to be dependent on the collection of minor forest produce to a large extent. Therefore, attempts should be made by the Forest Department to involve the Lodhas in the Joint Forest Management related activities and also to ensure their rights to forest under the new Forest Rights Act, 2006.

Fourth, the Lodha families to whom *patta* land have been issued on paper should immediately be given the actual right of possession with full protection against all kinds of disturbance by the district administration and the panchayat. The Government land departments should take initiative in the context of the ground reality of the vest land before their distribution as *pattas*.

The Lodha families who are cultivating on *patta* land but does not possess agricultural implements and bullocks should be given those items with proper arrangement of training by the concerned department of the Government.

Fifth, the financial assistance for house construction, which has been built for the Lodhas in the three administrative blocks, did not seem to be sustainable. The Lodhas were living within it but not with satisfaction. In some cases the roofs were found to be leaking. Moreover, the walls did not seem to be strong enough to stand for three to four years and if they required repair the Lodhas would not be able to do it without the help of the contractors. So, it would have been better if by spending a lesser amount of money the houses were built by using their own labour and indigenous raw materials for the walls (clay) and the roof (tiles, straw etc) under the supervision of trained Government officials of the Planning and Development Department of the District. The financial assistance for house construction plans should also have been made in consultation with the beneficiaries themselves to give honour and importance to their specific needs.

Sixth, and not the least, solar cells should not be given to individual Lodha families without enquiring into their socioeconomic conditions. This of course does not mean that solar cells should never be given to individual Lodha families. In our research we have found that the Lodha families in the Narayangarh block were much advanced in terms of the utilization of the development inputs. Solar cell s should have been given to the Lodha families of this block instead of giving them to the beneficiaries in the Binpur II block.

The academic administrator and former District Magistrate of Paschim (west) Medinipur, Mr. Chandan Sinha narrated the successes of the Lodha development scheme in a positive tone. In the chapter ‘A Glow in the Darkness’ in his recently published book *Kindling of an Insurrection: Notes from Junglemahals*, Sinha depicted a good number of Lodha families in Jhargram who showed remarkable strength and courage at the individual and community levels to care for the poultry and the livestock given to them by the Government under the RSVY scheme and built houses under a governmental scheme with their family labour. In Sinha’s words:

> ... Darkness had fallen but with the help of torchlight we made our way to the house of Hari and Pramila Sabar. Upon reaching their homestead I found Hari Sabar digging one side of the foundation all by himself! I asked him why he was working so late. He told me that during the day he had gone to the jungle to collect sal leaves. Upon his return finding some portion of the foundation incomplete he decided to

> complete digging the length before calling it a day. It was stirring sight, especially since most people tend to dismiss Lodhas as incapable of hard work and responsibility. (Sinha, 2013:206-208).

The lessons which we have learned while working in the impact assessment study on the Lodhas under the RSVY scheme was no less revealing than Chandan Sinha 's experience. While Sinha learned from the Lodhas, we learned from the engineers who constructed rainwater harvesting tanks for the poor Lodha villagers. Let us narrate our experience.

With huge funding from the Central Government under the Rastriya Sam Vikas Yojna (RSVY) Scheme, which we have mentioned in the earlier chapters rainwater harvesting tanks were being excavated in the Binpur II block (these areas later became strongholds of the Maoists) of our study area. It is tempting to narrate the experience of two such recently excavated rainwater harvesting tanks in a mouza village named Sankhabhanga about 20kms from Belpahari block Headquarters on the way towards the Dhalbhumgarh district of the Jharkhand state. We have already described this village. We saw these tanks in 2005. Both these rainwater harvesting tanks were dug at a high elevation and there was hardly any water in those tanks. About five lakh rupees had been spent under the RSVY Scheme to dig up the 50 ft X 30ft X 12ft tanks at Sankhabhanga which was inhabited by poor Santal, Munda and a few Lodha families for their economic upliftment. The villagers got daily wages in the excavation work and we found during our fieldwork that some of the relatively better off families (non-Lodhas) were thinking of growing fish in the tank. Since the tanks were excavated on a high elevation there was hardly any chance that the tanks would be able to retain rainwater. After enquiry with the engineers of the concerned department of the district on the choice of the site for these tanks we learnt that under the RSVY scheme it was mandatory to excavate such tanks on land voluntarily donated by Scheduled Tribe or Scheduled Caste families to ensure better participation by the villagers. The engineers frankly admitted that usually one donates the worst type of land for tanks, which would be used for communal purposes in future and they reminded us to add with it the fact that the quality of land normally possessed by the Scheduled Tribe and Scheduled Caste families happened to be of inferior quality than those owned by the higher castes in the villages. Moreover, the engineers admitted 'We had to excavate those tanks within the 2004-2005 financial years to fulfill our target'! (Guha, 2010). This was how macro-level policy categories operated on micro-level realities.

APPENDICES

Appendix A.

Particulars of Patta Record and Related Information on The Lodha/Sabar Families of Binpur-II & Nayagram Blocks of Paschim Medinipur

Sl.No	Name of Household Head	Block and G. P	Mouza with J.L no	Details of patta record	Reason of inability for cultivation and other problems regarding cultivation
1.	Raghu Sabar	Binpur-II, Simul pal	Sankhabhanga, 157	Plot no. 1/373 Area-.09 acre Date of issue-29.06.91	Not yet seen the plot
2.	Chunu Sabar	Binpur-II, Simul pal	Sankhabhanga, 157	Plot no. 1/373 Area-.08 acre Date of issue-29.06.91	Not yet seen the plot
3.	Surendra Sabar	Binpur-II, Simul pal	Sankhabhanga, 157	Plot no. 20/399 Area-.42 acre Date of issue-29.06.91	Not yet seen the plot
4.	Rabi Sabar	Binpur-II, Banspahari	Chakadoba 13	The informant reported that the patta was issued but he lost it.	Does not know about the plot.
5.	Swapan Sabar	Binpur-II, Banspahari	Chakadoba 13	The informant reported that the patta was issued but he lost it.	Does not know about the plot.
6.	Mangal Sabar	Binpur-II, Banspahari	Amlashol 25	Plot no.193 Area- 0.93 acre Date of issue-6.12.05	Could not say anything.

Sl.No	Name of Household Head	Block and G. P	Mouza with J.L no	Details of patta record	Reason of inability for cultivation and other problems regarding cultivation
7.	Late Sukra Sabar(patta was issued against his name) Kanu Sabar(S/O late Sukra Sabar.He now possesses the patta paper)	Binpur-II, Banspahari	Amlashol 25	Plot no. 70, 148, 117,182,246,235 Area-0.42 acar Date of issue-6.12.05	The patta was issued in favour of his father late Sukra Sabar. But he could not cultivate these land because former land holder is cultivating on it by fource
8.	Late Samba Sabar(patta was issued against his name) Radhu Sabar(S/O late Samba Sabar.He now possesses the patta paper)	Binpur-II Banspahari	Amlashol 25	PlotNo: 206,203 Area:0.60 acar Date of issue 6.12.05	The patta was issued in favour of his father late Samba Sabar. But he could not cultivate these land because former land holder is cultivating on it by fource
9.	Jiban Sabar	Binpur-II Banspahari	Amlashol 25	Area:0.15 acre	Not yet seen the plot
10.	Kotal Sabar	Binpur-II Simulpal	Rimradanga 90	Plot No:64 Area:0.94 acre Date of issue:23.4.97	Cultivate this land
11.	Ramani Digar	Nayagram, Kharikamathani	Ambishol 115	Plot nos. 185, 67, 164, 211, 179, 210, 120 Area-3.11 acres.	Does not possess plough and bullocks. So hires them at the rate of Rs 70-80 per day.
12.	Ntabar Digar	Nayagram, Kharikamathani	Ambishol 115	Plot no. 66 Area-.59 acres Date of issue 29. 11. 94.	Could not cultivate the land because he does not possess plough and bullocks.
Sl.No	**Name of Household Head**	**Block and G. P**	**Mouza with J.L no**	**Details of patta record**	**Reason of inability for cultivation and other problems regarding cultivation**

Appendix A. (Continued)

13.	Panchanan Digar	Nayagram, Kharikamathani	Ambishol 115	Plot nos- 67,182, 211, 179, 213, 120, 212. Area-.38 acres. Date of issue- 5.2.95	The patta was issued in favour of his father Late Ananta Digar. But could not cultivate since other persons are cultivating on it by force.
14.	Lakhindar Digar	Nayagram, Kharikamathani	Ambishol 115	Plot no 148 Area-.33 acre Date of issue-10.10.93	The plot yields two crops in a year. Hires plough and bullocks from father-in- law's house who is a Santal.
15.	Jiten Digar	Nayagram, Kharikamathani	Ambishol 115	Plot no- 66/282 Area-.71 acres	Hires plough and bullocks from his elder brother Natabar.
16	Basanta Digar	Nayagram, Kharikamathani	Ambishol 115	Plot nos-43,118 (Homestead) Area- 1.61 acres	Hires plough and bullocks from Neighbour.
17.	Duari Bhakta	Nayagram, Kharikamathani	Ambishol 115	The informant did not show the patta.	The informant reported that patta was issued but other persons were cultivating on the land.
18.	Manglu Bhakta	Nayagram, Kharikamathani	Ambishol 115	The informant did not show the patta.	Dose not cultivating the land lack of Agricultural implements.
19.	Susanta Bhakta	Nayagram, Kharikamathani	Ambishol 115	The informant reported that the patta was issued but he lost it.	Other persons were cultivating on the land.

Sl.No	Name of Household Head	Block and G. P	Mouza with J.L no	Details of patta record	Reason of inability for cultivation and other problems regarding cultivation
13.	Panchanan Digar	Nayagram, Kharikamathani	Ambishol 115	Plot nos- 67,182, 211, 179, 213, 120, 212. Area-.38 acres. Date of issue- 5.2.95	The patta was issued in favour of his father Late Ananta Digar. But could not cultivate since other persons are cultivating on it by force.
20.	Naren Digar	Nayagram, Kharikamathani	Ambishol 115	The informant reported that the patta was issued.He did not show it.	Does not possess plough and bullocks. Given the patta land to other person on share.
21.	Chhotomangal Digar	Nayagram, Kharikamathani	Ambishol 115	The informant reported that the patta was issued.He did not show it.	Other persons were cultivating on the land.
22.	Sona Bhakta	Nayagram, Kharikamathani	Bankshol 111	Plot no-61 Area-.10 acre Year of issue 1998.	Does not know about the land.
23.	Gura Bhakta	Nayagram, Kharikamathani	Bankshol 111	The informant reported that the patta was issued.He did not show it.	Does not know about the land.
24.	Paria Bhakta	Nayagram, Kharikamathani	Bankshol 111	Plot no-61 Area-.10 acre Year of issue 1997.	Does not know about the land.

Appendix A. (Continued)

Sl.No	Name of Household Head	Block and G. P	Mouza with J.L no	Details of patta record	Reason of inability for cultivation and other problems regarding cultivation
25.	Nakul Bhakta	Nayagram Sitalpur	Sitalpur	Plot no-112,87 Area-.50 acre Date of issue 17.12.97.	Does not possess plough and bullocks and the quality of the land is very poor. Does not cultivate.
26.	Baishakhi Bhakta	Nayagram Sitalpur	Sitalpur	The informant reported that the patta was issued but he lost it.	Does not cultivate.
27.	Khagen Bhakta	Nayagram Sitalpur	Sitalpur	The informant reported that the patta was issued for.12 acre but did not show it.	Does not possess plough and bullocks and the quality of the land is very poor. Does not cultivate.
28.	Rabindra Bhakta	Nayagram Sitalpur	Sitalpur	Plot no-49,89 Area-.35 acre.	Cultivates with hired Plough and bullocks.
29.	Bhutnath Mallik	Nayagram Kalmapukuria	Bansiashol 116	Plot nos-87,156,61 Area- 1.07 acre. Date of issue 8.9.93	Cultivates by hired plough and bullocks.
30.	Suren Mallik	Nayagram Kalmapukuria	Bansiashol 116	Plot nos-20,23 Area-.50 acre.	Cultivates by hired plough and bullocks
31.	Bainu Bhunia	Nayagram Palasia	Palasia	The informant reported that the patta was issued but did not show it.	Other persons were cultivating on the land.

APPENDIX B. A FACSIMILE OF THE DISTRICT MAGISTRATE'S LETTER OF PASCHIM MEDINIPUR

নারায়ণ স্বরূপ নিগম, আই.এ.এস.
জেলা শাসক ও জেলা সমাহর্তা
পশ্চিম মেদিনীপুর
পোষ্ট - মেদিনীপুর - ৭২১১০১, পশ্চিমবঙ্গ

সত্যমেব জয়তে

Narayan Swaroop Nigam, I.A.S.
District Magistrate & Collector
Paschim Medinipur
P.O. Midnapore - 721101, West Bengal
Off. : (03222) 275571
Resi. : (03222) 275570
Fax : (03222) 275427
E-mail : dm-mid@wb.nic.in

D. O. No. *164*

Date *22-02-2010*

Dear Prof Guha,

I thankfully acknowledge the receipt of your papers. It is a very interesting reading definitely for development inputs among the Lodha communities and problems in implementation of different schemes.

Please do share with me any future report as well.

With regards. *Yours faithfully*

(Narayan Swaroop Nigam)

Shri Abhijit Guha,
Reader,
Department of Anthropology,
Vidyasagar University,
Midnapore.

Appendix C. News Item Published in *The Statesman*

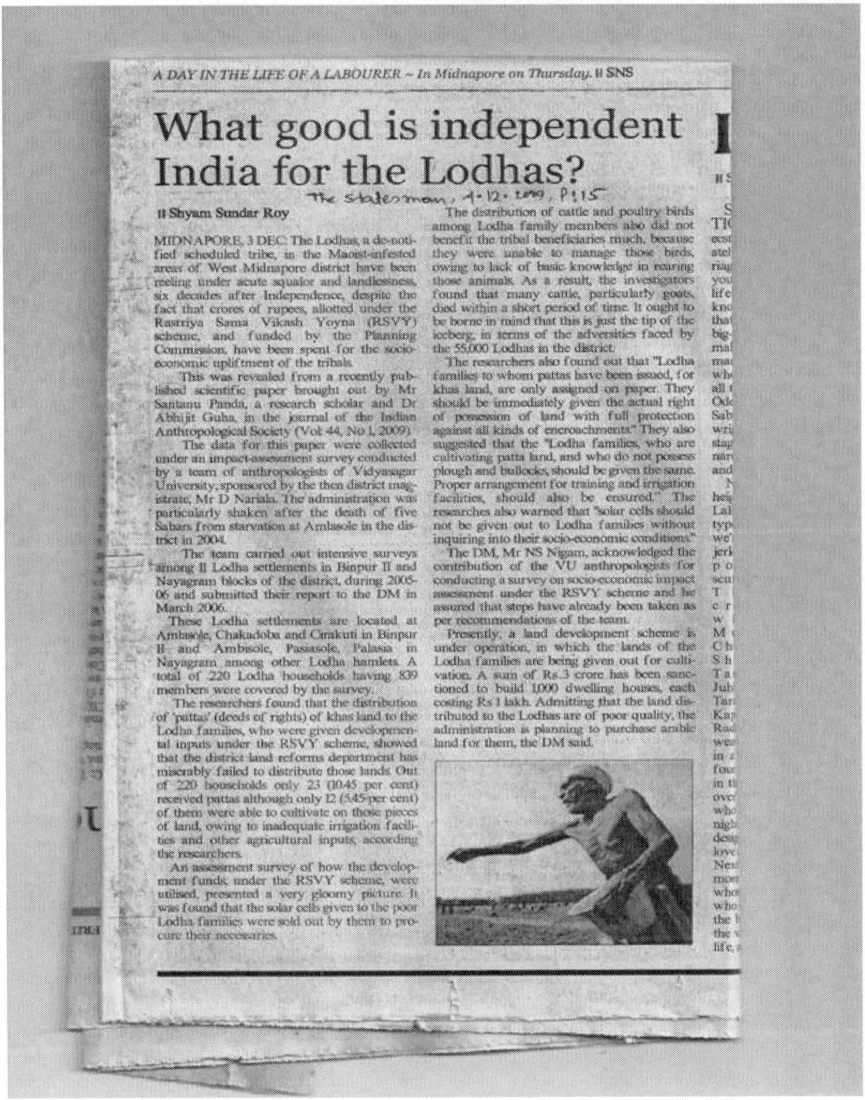

A DAY IN THE LIFE OF A LABOURER ~ In Midnapore on Thursday. ‖ SNS

What good is independent India for the Lodhas?

The Statesman, 4.12.2009, P.15

‖ Shyam Sundar Roy

MIDNAPORE, 3 DEC: The Lodhas, a de-notified scheduled tribe, in the Maoist-infested areas of West Midnapore district have been reeling under acute squalor and landlessness, six decades after Independence, despite the fact that crores of rupees, allotted under the Rastriya Sama Vikash Yoyna (RSVY) scheme, and funded by the Planning Commission, have been spent for the socio-economic upliftment of the tribals.

This was revealed from a recently published scientific paper brought out by Mr Santanu Panda, a research scholar and Dr Abhijit Guha, in the journal of the Indian Anthropological Society (Vol 44, No 1, 2009).

The data for this paper were collected under an impact-assessment survey conducted by a team of anthropologists of Vidyasagar University, sponsored by the then district magistrate, Mr D Narială. The administration was particularly shaken after the death of five Sabars from starvation at Amlasole in the district in 2004.

The team carried out intensive surveys among 11 Lodha settlements in Binpur II and Nayagram blocks of the district, during 2005-06 and submitted their report to the DM in March 2006.

These Lodha settlements are located at Amlasole, Chakadoba and Cirakuti in Binpur II and Ambisole, Pasiasole, Palasia in Nayagram among other Lodha hamlets. A total of 220 Lodha households having 839 members were covered by the survey.

The researchers found that the distribution of 'pattas' (deeds of rights) of khas land to the Lodha families, who were given developmental inputs under the RSVY scheme, showed that the district land reforms department has miserably failed to distribute those lands. Out of 220 households only 23 (10.45 per cent) received pattas although only 12 (5.45 per cent) of them were able to cultivate on those pieces of land, owing to inadequate irrigation facilities and other agricultural inputs, according the researchers.

An assessment survey of how the development funds, under the RSVY scheme, were utilised, presented a very gloomy picture. It was found that the solar cells given to the poor Lodha families were sold out by them to procure their necessaries.

The distribution of cattle and poultry birds among Lodha family members also did not benefit the tribal beneficiaries much, because they were unable to manage those birds, owing to lack of basic knowledge in rearing those animals. As a result, the investigators found that many cattle, particularly goats, died within a short period of time. It ought to be borne in mind that this is just the tip of the iceberg, in terms of the adversities faced by the 55,000 Lodhas in the district.

The researchers also found out that "Lodha families to whom pattas have been issued, for khas land, are only assigned on paper. They should be immediately given the actual right of possession of land with full protection against all kinds of encroachments." They also suggested that the "Lodha families, who are cultivating patta land, and who do not possess plough and bullocks, should be given the same. Proper arrangement for training and irrigation facilities, should also be ensured." The researches also warned that "solar cells should not be given out to Lodha families without inquiring into their socio-economic conditions."

The DM, Mr NS Nigam, acknowledged the contribution of the VU anthropologists for conducting a survey on socio-economic impact assessment under the RSVY scheme and he assured that steps have already been taken as per recommendations of the team.

Presently, a land development scheme is under operation, in which the lands of the Lodha families are being given out for cultivation. A sum of Rs.3 crore has been sanctioned to build 1,000 dwelling houses, each costing Rs 1 lakh. Admitting that the land distributed to the Lodhas are of poor quality, the administration is planning to purchase arable land for them, the DM said.

APPENDIX D. DEVELOPMENTAL SCHEMES IMPLEMENTED BY THE GOVERNMENT

IAY (Indira Awas Yojana)

This scheme started operation since 1985. It is a Government of India social welfare programme to provide housing for the rural poor in India. It is one of the major flagship programs of the Rural Development Ministry to construct houses for BPL population in the villages. Under the scheme, financial assistance worth Rs. 45000/- in plain areas and Rs. 48500/- in difficult areas (high land area) is provided for construction of houses. The houses are allotted in the name of the woman or jointly between husband and wife. The construction of the houses is the sole responsibility of the beneficiary and engagement of contractors is strictly prohibited.

The broad purpose of the scheme is to provide financial assistance to some of the weakest sections of society for them to upgrade or construct a house of respectable quality for their personal living. The vision of the Government is to replace all temporary (*kutchcha*) houses from Indian villages by 2017 (en.wikipedia.org/wiki/Indira_Awaas_Yojana. Accessed on 09.11.2012)

ICDS (Integrated Child Development Services)

Launched on 2nd October 1975, today, ICDS Scheme represents one of the world's largest and most unique programmes for early childhood development. ICDS is the foremost symbol of India 's commitment to her children – India's response to the challenge of providing pre-school education on one hand and breaking the vicious cycle of malnutrition, morbidity, reduced learning capacity and mortality, on the other.The Integrated Child Development Services (ICDS) Scheme was launched in 1975 with the following objectives:

a. to improve the nutritional and health status of children in the age - group 0-6 years;
b. to lay the foundation for proper psychological, physical and social development of the child;
c. to reduce the incidence of mortality, morbidity, malnutrition and school dropout;

d. to achieve effective co-ordination of policy and implementation amongst the various departments to promote child development; and
e. to enhance the capability of the mother to look after the normal health and nutritional needs of the child through proper nutrition and health education.

The above objectives are sought to be achieved through a package of services comprising:

a. supplementary nutrition,
b. immunization,
c. health check-up,
d. referral services,
e. pre-school non-formal education and
f. Nutrition and health education. *(wcd.nic.in/icds.htm. Accessed on 12.11.2012).*

ITDP (Integrated Tribal Development Project)

The Ministry of Tribal Affairs releases grant to the State Government s for the implementation of the schemes/programmes for Scheduled Tribes meant for their socio-economic development and protection against exploitation. There are 192 Integrated Tribal Development Project (ITDPs)/Integrated Tribal Development Agencies (ITDAs) spread over 19 States/Union Territories in the country. The concerned State Governments implement these schemes/programme by releasing funds to their administrative units viz. ITDPs/ITDAs etc. and details of funding and implementation of items of work of these schemes/programmes, are maintained by these States. Since the responsibility of monitoring their administrative units, also rests with the State, such details are not maintained in the Ministry. (*pib.nic.in/release/release.asp?relid=82621. Accessed on 12.11.2012).*

MGNREGA (Mahatma Gandhi National Rural Employment Guarantee Act)

The scheme was launched on February 2, 2006 from Anantapur in Andhra Pradesh and initially covered 200 "poorest" districts of the country. The Act was implemented in phased manner – 130 districts were added in 2007–08. With its spread over 625 districts across the country, the flagship program of the UPA Government has the potential to increase the purchasing power of rural poor, reduce distress migration and to create useful assets in rural India. Also, it can foster social and gender equality as 23% workers under the scheme are Scheduled Castes, 17% Scheduled Tribes and 50% women. In 2010–11, 41 million households were employed on NREGA worksites. This Act was introduced with an aim of improving the purchasing power of the rural people, primarily semi or un-skilled work to people living in rural India, whether or not they are below the poverty line. (en.wikipedia.org/.../ Mahatma_Gandhi_National_Rural_Employment...Accessed on: 09.11.2012)

PMGSY (Pradhan Mantri Gram Sadak Yojana)

The PMGSY is a nationwide plan in India to provide good all-weather road connectivity to unconnected villages. It is under the authority of the Ministry of Rural Development and began on 25 December 2000.

The goal was to provide roads to all villages (1) with a population of 1000 persons and above by 2003, (2) with a population of 500 persons and above by 2007, (3) in hill states, tribal and desert area villages with a population of 500 persons and above by 2003, and (4) in hill states, tribal and desert area villages with a population of 250 persons and above by 2007. (http://en.wikipedia.org/ wiki/Pradhan_Mantri_Gram_Sadak_Yojana Downloaded on 09.11.2012)

RSVY (Rastriya Sama Vikas Yojana)

The scheme was launched during the period 2004-2005. The scheme aimed at focused development programmes for backward areas which would help reduce imbalances and speed up development.Under the RSVY scheme, the Central Government aimed to cover 100 backward districts in India. Already 50 backward districts have been covered during 2003-2004 and a sum of Rs.15000 crore per year was provided to each of the district for a period of three years, that is a total of Rs. 45.00 crore per district have been released to the State Government s on hundred percent grant basis in installment. The plan document revealed that the main objective of the RSVY scheme would be to address the problems of low agricultural productivity, unemployment in the rural areas, and to fill in the critical gaps in the physical and social infrastructure s of the 'Backward region'. There is a scope in the scheme to make plans to improve the socio-economic conditions of the 'poorer pockets' and/or specific disadvantaged groups and communities. (RSVY, Planning Commission doc. Govt. of India Downloaded on 06.07.2011)

SGRY (Sampoorna Grameen Rozgar Yojana)

The scheme was a scheme launched by the Government of India to attain the objective of providing gainful employment for the rural poor. From 1 April 1999, EAS became an allocation-based scheme. The programme was implemented through the Panchayati Raj institutions.

The Sampoorna Grameen Rozgar Yojana was launched on 25 September 2001 by merging the provisions of Employment Assurance Scheme (EAS) and Jawahar Samridhi Yojana (JGSY). The programme is self-targeting in nature and aims to provide employment and food to people in rural areas who lived below the poverty line.

The Sampoorna Grameen Rozgar Yojana is actually a combination of the provisions under the Employment Assurance Scheme (EAS) and Jawahar Gram Samridhi Yojana (JGSY).

The scheme has following objectives:

1. To provide additional wage employment in rural areas.
2. To provide food security.
3. To create durable community, social and economic infrastructure in rural areas.
4. Special emphasis to provide Wage Employment to:-
    a. Women
    b. Scheduled caste
    c. Scheduled Tribes.
    d. Parents of children withdrawn from hazardous occupations.
    e. (*en.wikipedia.org/wiki/Sampoorna_Grameen_Rozgar_Yojana* Downloaded on 09.11.2012).

APPENDIX E. PHOTOGRAPHS

Plate I Facing Sankhabhanga Village of Binpur-II block.

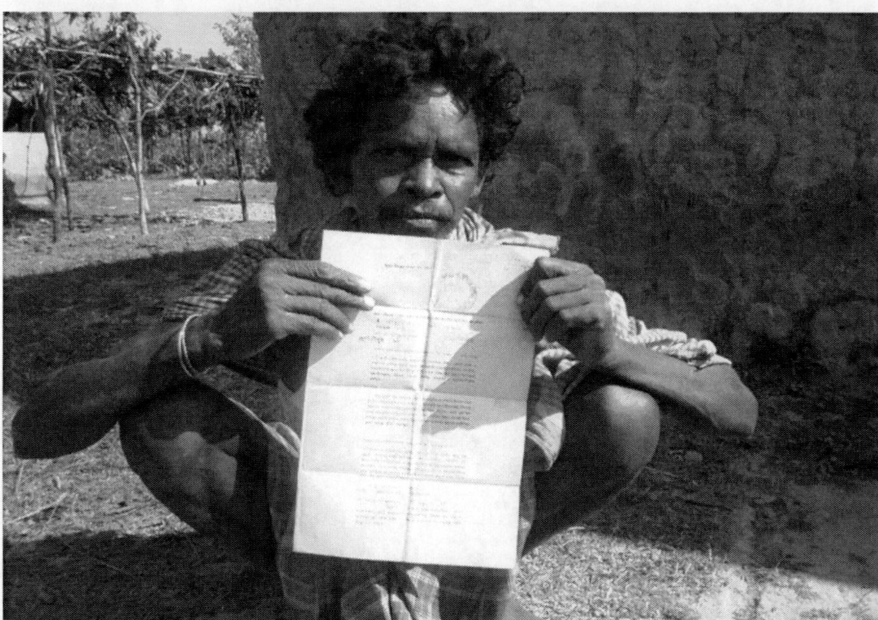

Plate II. A landless Lodha showing his patta record who had never seen his plot.

Plate III. Lodha women of Nayagram with her goats received from the Government.

Plate IV. Solar cell s on the rooftop of a Lodha beneficiary at Nayagram block.

Plate V. First author with informants at Palasia village in Nayagram block.

Plate VI. A house constructed by the Government for a Lodha family in Narayangarh block.

Plate VII. A Lodha farmer spraying insecticide in his own agricultural land in Daharpur village at Narayangarh.

Plate VIII. An incomplete house constructed with mud & bricks under the IAY.

Plate IX. Lodha Children sharing food in Amlasole village at Binpur II.

Plate X. The rainwater harvesting pond at Sankhabhanga village.

Plate XI. Solar cell kept at an unprotected place in front of the house of a Lodha beneficiary at Nayagram.

Plate XII. Lodha women stitching the Sal leafs to prepare plates in Nayagram.

Plate XIII. Lodha woman making ropes with Babui grass in Nayagram.

Plate XIV. The authors interviewing (2nd and 3rd from the left) a Lodha woman making rope with Babui grass in Binpur II.

Plate XV. Lodha women carrying firewood collected from the forest at Nayagram covering about 5 kms.

GLOSSARY

Babui A kind of grass which grows in the dry forest zones and used for making ropes. The scientific name of this grass is *Eulalopsis* binata.

Gram Panchayat The third tier of elected local self government in West Bengal consisting of several *mouza* villages.

Gram Samsad The fourth tier of elected panchayats in West Bengal which operates at the *mouza* level.

Hat The weekly local market in Indian villages.

Jungle Mahal literally 'jungle estates', was a district formed by British colonialists in India and some independent chiefdoms lying between Birbhum, Bankura, Midnapore and the hilly country of Chota Nagpur in what is now the Indian state of West Bengal.

Kharif A rice of crop of Bengal sown in November and harvested in February.

Kendu leaf It is leaf of Kendu tree (*Diospyros melanoxylon*) used for making local cigarettes in India.

Mouza A revenue unit bearing a local name which may or may not overlap with the village defined by the people.

Paan It is the leaf of vine belonging to the Betel (*Piper betle*). It is valued both as a mild stimulant and for its medicinal properties.

Para A smaller subdivision having a cultural and physical boundary within a village

Patta Land given to landless families by the Government with the help of the Land and Landa Reforms Act 1955. Patta land can be inherited but can not be sold.

Pradhan The head of the statutory gram panchayat (lowest level of the three tier Local Self Government.

Rabi A variety of crops including wheat, pulses and winter vegetables sown after the rainy season.

Shishu Sikha Kendra It is a village based non-formal school funded by the Government

Tussore A kind of thread which develops in the body of an insect (*Bombyx mori*) and used for making clothes.

References

Abrahum, S. 1999. Steal or I'll Call You a Thief: 'Criminal' Tribes of India. Economic and Political Weakly, Vol. 34. No. 27: 1751-1753.

Agnihotri, Satish. 2000. *Sex ratio patterns in the Indian population:* A Fresh Exploration. Sage: New Delhi.

Amnesty International Report, 2001. pp: 1-51.

Basu, Soma. 2012. Brutal inheritance. *The Sunday Statesman,* 26 August 2012, p. 1.

Bera, Nalini. 2005. *Sabar Charit.* Kolkata: Karuna Prakashani.

Bernard, H.R. 1994. *Research Methods in Anthropology: Qualitative and Quantitative Approaches.* Thousand Oaks, CA: Sage Publications.

Béteille, André. 1986. The concept of tribe with special reference to India. European Journal of Sociology, Vol 27, Issue 2, pp 296-318. doi:10.1017/S000397560000463X.

Bhottacharjo, D. 1992. Chuni Kotal er Attohota (The Suicide of Chuni Kotal), "Amader Progotir Mukhosh Khule Dilen Chuni Kotal, Tanr Jibon Diye" (By Losing Her Life, Chuni Kotal Has Taken Away Our Progressive Mask) Kolkata: *Anandabazar Patrika*, 20 August 1992.

Bhowmick P.K. 1961. "Four Midnapore Villages", in *West Bengal, District Census Hand book, Midnapore* Volume II: 3-47.

Bhowmick P.K. 1966. '*Proceedings of the summer school in Anthropology' Ed. by* N.C. Choudhury. Darjeeling: Anthropological Survey of India.

Bhowmick P.K. 1981. Rehabilitaion of a 'Denotified Community ' The Ex-Criminal Lodhas of West Bengal. *Royal Anthropological Institute Newsletter*. 44: 6-8.

Bhowmick P.K. 1985. Tribal Situation West Bengal, *The Anthropologist*, vol. 15, No.1, pp: 1-19.

Bhowmick, Probodh Kumar. 1994. *The Lodhas of West Bengal.* Kolkata: Institute of Social Research and Applied Anthropology (ISRAA).

Bisai, S. Bose, K,and Ghosh, A. 2008. Prevalence of Undernutrition of Lodha Children Aged 1-14 Years of Paschim Medinipur District, West Bengal, India. *Iranian Journal of Pediatrics.* 18 (4): 323-329.

Bisai, S. Bose, K. and Ghosh, A. 2008. Nutritional Status of Lodha Children in a Village of Paschim Medinipur District, West Bengal. *Indian Journal of Public Health.* 52 (4): 203-206.

Bose K, Bisai. S, Mondal, P.S. and Ghosh, M. 2008. Body mass index and chronic energy deficiency among adult male Lodhas and Bhumijs: A comparison with other tribal populations of West Bengal. *Indian Journal of Public Health.* 16 (2): 117-121.

Chanda, A. 2005. Tribal Women, in *The Changing Status of Women in West Bengal, 1970-2000 the Challenge Ahead.* Edited by J. Bagchi, pp.130-141. Sage Publications: New Delhi.

Chatterjee, D., Ghosh, S., Sen, S. 2002.*Human Rights: Theory and Practice.* South Asian Publishers: Kolkata.

Chattopadhyay, P. and Das, A. K.2006. The changing role of individuals in the death rituals of the Lodhas of Kharagpur, in *Anthropology of Primitive Tribes in India. Edited by P. Das Sharma.* Serials: New Delhi.

Danda, A.K.2002. 'Predicaments of a marginalized community: The Lodha ' *Journal of Anthropological Survey of India.* 51: 103-111.

Devi Mahasveta. 1983. *Lodhas of West Bengal -1.* Economic and Political Weekly. Vol. 18. N0. 22: 947-949.

Devi Mahasveta. 1985. The Savara Tribals of West Bengal 1- Shavaras of Midnapur. *Economic and Political Weekly,* Vol. 20. N0. 35: 1467-1469.

Devi Mahasveta. 1992. The story of Chuni Kotal. *Economic and Political Weekly*, Vol. XVII, N0. 35, P-1836-1837.

Devy, G. 2000. For a Nomad called thief, *India International Centre Quaterly*, vol. 27, No. 2 Marginalised, pp: 51-60.

Devy, G.N. 'The Branded Tribes of India '. *Peoples' Union of Civil Liberties Bulletin.* September, 1998.

Dhrgupta, A. Goswami, A. Sen, M. and Mazumder, D. 2009. Study on the Effect of Socio-economic Parameters on Health Status of the Toto, Santal, Sabar and Lodha Tribes of West Bengal, India. *Tribes and Tribal.* 7(1): 31-38.

District Human Development Report: Paschim Medinipur. 2011. Development & Planning Department, Government of West Bengal: Kolkata.

District Statistical Handbook. 2006. *Paschim Medinipur*. Bureau of Applied Economics and Statistics, Government of West Bengal: Calcutta.

Duary, N. K and Haldar, A.K. 2006. Education among the Lodha of West Bengal, in *Anthropology of Primitive Tribes in India.* Edited by P. Das Sharma. Serials: New Delhi.

Duary, N.K. 2005. "Economy and Education among the PTGs in West Bengal ", in *Primitive Tribes in Contemporary India: Concept, Ethnography and Demography*, Volume 1. Edited by S.K. Choudhuri and S.S. Choudhuri, pp. 297-314. Mittal Publications: New Delhi.

Faulkner, L. P. 1923. Settlements of Criminal Tribes of India. *Journal of the Royal Society of Arts*. Vol.71, No.3677, pp: 449.

Faulkner, L. P. 1923. Settlements of Criminal Tribes of India. *Journal of the Royal Society of Arts*. Vol.71, No.3677, pp: 449.

Guha, A. 2010. Alwar shows the way. *Frontier*, Vol. 42 No. 29, Jan 31-Feb 6.

Mandal, H. et.al. 2002. West Bengal, in *India: An Illustrated Atlas of Tribal World*. Anthropological Survey of India: Kolkata.

Mitra, A. 1953. The Tribes and castes of West Bengal: Census 1951. *Calcutta: Land and Land Revenue Department Govt. of West Bengal*.

Narayan, S. 1988. *Indian Anthropology*. Delhi: Gayan Publishing House.

Panda, S. 2010. Problem of women self-help-groups among the Lodhas of Daharpur village in Paschim Medinipur, West Bengal, in *Ecology of Bio-cultural Perspectives in India.* Edited by S. Mondal, S. Bhui and N. Mandal. Mahishadal Girls College, pp. 59-72.

Panda, S. 2010. Sex- ratio pattern among the Lodhas of Paschim Medinipur, West Bengal. Indian *Journal of Biological Sciences*. 16:39-46.

Panda, S. and Guha, A. 2009. Development Inputs among the Lodhas in a District of WestBengal: Problems of Implementation and Recommendations. *Journal of the Indian Anthropological Society*. 44: 69-75.

Panda, S. and Guha, A. 2012 Ground realities of development among the Lodhas in West Bengal. *Journal of South Asian Anthropologist,* Vol. 13. 75-84.

Panda, S. and Guha, A. 2013 The Lodhas of West Bengal: A case study. *The Tribal Tribune*. (Online journal ISSN: 2249-3433), Vol.6, Issue 2(2014).

Panda, S. and Guha, A. 2013. Micro-categories of Development and Micro-level Realities: A Case Study of Lodhas in Paschim Medinipur, West Bengal. *Journal of the Indian Anthropological Society*. Vol.48, pp. 245-255.

Pramanick Paramananda.2009. *Adibasi Sanskritir Ruparekha*. Kolkata: Fire Dekha Prakashani.

Radhakrishna, M. 2009. Starvation among Primitive Tribal Groups. *Economic and Political Weekly,* Vol. 40. No. 18, pp: 13-16.

Report on the Assessment of the Impact of Developmental Programmes on the Socioeconomic Condition of the Lodha/Sabar Community of Binpur II & Nayagram Block of Paschim Medinipur, 2006. (Unpublished): Department of Anthropology, Vidyasagar University. [Available at: https://www.academia.edu/5522826/Report_on_the_assessment _of_the_impact_of_developmental_programmes_on_the_socioeconomic_condition_of_the_Lodha_Sabar_community _of_BinpurII_and_Nayagram_blocks_of_Paschim_Medinipur_West_Bengal_India].

Roy, Shyam Sundar. 2009. What good is Independent India for the Lodhas? *The Statesman,* 4 December 2009, p. 15.

Sahlins, M. D. 1968. *Tribesman*. Englewood Cliffs, New Jersey: Prentice-Hall, Sinha, Chandan. 2013 *Kindling of an Insurrection: Notes from Jungle Mahal s.* Routledge.

Singh, Kumar, Suresh. 1994 *People of India: The Scheduled Tribes.* Oxford University Press: Anthropological Survey of India.

Sinha, Chandan. 2013 *Kindling of an Insurrection: Notes from Jungle Mahal s.* Routledge.

Sinha, S. 1958. Tribal Cultures of Peninsular India as a Dimension of Little Tradition in the Study of Indian Civilisation: A Prelimiinary Statement. *Journal of American Folklore,* vol 71, July-September.

Starvation Death? A report from *Economic and Political Weekly*, 2004:2541.

Tiwari, D. K. Sharma. K.K.N. and Dubey, V.S. 2001. Health Profile among Lodha and Munda Tribal Children of Midnapur District, West Bengal. *Anthropologist*; 3(3): 189-190.

Tribal Health Bulletin (Special Issue), 2014. pp: 1-126.

Tucker, B. 1923. The Criminal Tribe of India, *Journal of the Royal Society of Arts*. Vol.71, No.3661, pp: 158-166.

Verma. R.C.1990. *Indian Tribes through the ages.* Ministry of Information and Broadcasting. Govt. of India.

Vidyarthi, Lalita Prasad.1978. *Rise of anthropology in India: a social science orientation Volume 1. The Tribal Dimensions..* Delhi: Concept Publishing Company.

Xaxa, Virginius. 1999. Transformation of Tribes in India: Terms of Discourse. *Economic and Political Weekly.* Vol. 34, No. 24, pp. 1519-1524.

Xaxa, Virginious. 1999. Tribes as Indigenous People of India. *Economic and Political Weekly*. Vol. 34, No. 51, pp. 3589-3595.

Webliography

http://en.wikipedia.org/wiki/Purulia _district
http://en.wikipedia.org/wiki/Politics_of_West_Bengal
en.wikipedia.org/wiki/Indira_Awaas_Yojana. Accessed on 09.11.2012
en.wikipedia.org/.../Mahatma_Gandhi_National_Rural_Employment...Accesse d on: 09.11.2012.
en.wikipedia.org/wiki/Sampoorna_Grameen_Rozgar_Yojana Downloaded on 09.11.2012.
http://www.maplandia.com/india/west-bengal/medinipur/jhargram/railway-stations/famous-for-shal-tree/
http://en.wikipedia.org/wiki/Pradhan_Mantri_Gram_Sadak_Yojana *Downloaded on 09.11.2012*)
en.wikipedia.org/wiki/Criminal_Tribes_Act
https://www.indianfolklore.org/journals/index.php/Mukt/.../134(Reference of denotified tribes in
India, PDF) censusindia.gov.in/Tables_Published/SCST/dh_st_westbengal .pdf.
https://www.indianfolklore.org/journals/index.php/Mukt/.../134
pib.nic.in/release/release.asp?relid=82621. Accessed on 12.11.201
**https://www.indianfolklore.org/journals/index.php/Mukt/.../134 accessed on 12.12.2012*
RSVY, Planning Commission doc. Govt. of India Downloaded on 06.07.2011
www.jhargram.in/about_jhargram.php accessed on 07.02.2010
http://books.google.co.in/books?id=oG9_QkvmUKMC&printsec=frontcover&source=gbs_ge_summary_r&cad=0# (Dated: 12.12.2011)
http://www.jstor.org/stable/4408149?seq=2
www.cscsarchive.org:8081/MediaArchive/audience.../A0220053.pdf
wbplan.gov.in/docs/Handbook_2004/PaschimMedinapur.pdf
wcd.nic.in/icds.htm. Accessed on 12.11.2012
http://www.census2011.co.in/census/district/18-paschim-medinipur.html accessed on 12.10.2014
http://en.wikipedia.org/wiki/Criminal_Tribes_Act Accessed on 11.07.2014
http://en.wikipedia.org/wiki/Indira_Awaas_Yojana. Accessed on 09.11.2012
http://en.wikipedia.org/wiki/Criminal_Tribes_Act Accessed on 11.07.2014

http://www.pucl.org/from-archives/Dalit-tribal/branded-tribes.htm accessed on 03.08.2014

http://en.wikipedia.org/wiki/Lodha _people accessed on 05.08.2014

http://en.wikipedia.org/wiki/Chuni_Kotal accessed through Google on 22.10.2014

https://www.academia.edu/7125800/Report_of_the_Ganguly_Commission_of _Inquiry_Incident_of_Death_of_Smt.Chuni_Kotal_on_16th_August_199 2.On_27_August_1992_the_Governor _of_West_Bengal_ordered_an_enquiry_committee_to_probe _into_the_causes_of_her_death.This_is_the_unpublished_report_of_the_e nquiry_committee.

https://vidyasagar.academia.edu/AbhijitGuha/Chuni-Kotal-Archive.

http://www.midnapore.in/museum/bidisa_museum1.html.

Index

F

G

H

I

J

K

L

M

N

P

R

S

T

U

V

W